You Can Change the World

Action Handbook for the 21st Century

A Report from the Club of Budapest

by
Ervin Laszlo

Foreword by
Mikhail Gorbachev

Positive News Publishing Ltd

Ervin Laszlo
You Can Change the World
© Ervin Laszlo 2002

Book and Cover Design by Sarah Wilkinson

Cover Photograph © Albert Arnaud / Still Pictures

ISBN: 0-9543505-0-2

Published by Positive News Publishing Ltd,
5 Bicton Enterprise Centre, Clun, Shropshire, SY7 8NF, UK.
Tel: 01588 640 022 Fax: 01588 640 033
Email: office@positivenews.org.uk
Website: www.positivenews.org.uk
a not-for-profit company

Contents

Contents continued

Preface

The message conveyed in this handbook matured in my mind over the past two decades. When I left the United Nations after seven years of designing and coordinating research into the social and economic aspects of what, in the Club of Rome, we used to call the 'world problematique', I became more and more convinced that fundamental change will not come from 'above', from the elected or appointed leaders of contemporary societies, but must come from 'below', from the people who live in those societies. In the past few years this conviction was reinforced by two parallel developments: first, the need for change, which became ever more urgent, and second, the unfolding and intensification of the will to change in society at the grass-roots level.

The challenge in this opening decade of the 21st century is to sustain and guide the change that is already happening, so it can bring us to the threshold of a world where all people can live without marginalising or killing each other and destroying the environment. This poses two questions: first, *what is really at stake?* as Mikhail Gorbachev asks in his Introduction, and second, *what can I do to sustain and guide the change that is happening?*

I founded the Club of Budapest in the 1990s to bring together creative people with 'planetary consciousness' to come up with answers to these questions. In the past six months I have put down the answers that crystallised in my own mind.

Thus the book in the hands of the reader is not the usual review and discussion of local or global problems and outline of the envisaged solutions, but a handbook in the truest sense of the word: a book to be consulted as you and I, and likeminded people around us, seek to change the world. This task is no longer utopian for the world is highly unstable and hence changeable, moreover the momentum for change is growing. The task before us is to reinforce this momentum and inform it so it will head in a positive direction. For this we must become clear about what is at stake – which is the same as knowing why the world needs changing – and we must form an idea how we can go about sustaining and guiding change through our own thinking, our own life, and our own personal development.

This handbook is addressed to people willing and ready to be agents of change towards a better future. This means the young and openminded people of all ages. It has grown out of discussion with many people in many parts of the world, first of all my friends and colleagues of the Club of Budapest. I cannot thank all of them but wish to express my gratitude and appreciation in particular to those who have helped me develop the various drafts and editions of this book. In Italy they are Enrico Cheli, Nitamo Montecucco, Aleandro Tommasi, and Olivero Beha of the Club di Budapest Italia; in Germany Peter Spiegel of the international Secretariat of the Club of Budapest and Thomas Druyen of the Club of Budapest Deutschland; in Hungary Iván Vitányi, Mária Sági, Judit Kovács and Géza Bányay of the Club of Budapest

Hungary, and in Japan Masami and Hiroo Saionji of the Goi Foundation and Club of Budapest Japan. I am most grateful to Mikhail Gorbachev, Honorary Member and key supporter of the Club of Budapest, for writing an Introduction that highlights the nature and importance of the message conveyed in this book. I am delighted to acknowledge the efficient and meticulous work of the entire Positive News Publishing team, including the Global News Education Trust (Global NET). Further I take pleasure in acknowledging the outstanding collaboration of Shauna Crockett Burrows, Editor of Positive News, and of Jane Taylor, Associate Editor, designer Sarah Wilkinson and Frances Farrer who has worked closely with them in copy editing the text. I owe special thanks to Jane, who has received and read at least four different versions of the manuscript, studied each one of them, made valuable suggestions for improving and completing the text, and helped me develop the final version during two intense work-filled days on the terrace of my house in Tuscany. If the results still contain important omissions or incomplete information that is not for lack of advice and collaboration – it is my responsibility alone.

Montescudaio, Tuscany
July 2002

The Club of Budapest, founded in 1993 by Ervin Laszlo, is an informal association of globally and locally active opinion leaders in fields of art, science, religion, and culture. It is dedicated to the evolution of values, ethics and consciousness in the interest of a better future. It has headquarters in Budapest, Stuttgart, and Washington; and national Chapters in the USA, Canada, Mexico, Brazil, France, Germany, Italy, Austria, Hungary, India, Japan, China, and Samoa.

The Honorary Members

H.E. Dsingis AITMATOV
Writer

H.E. Oscar ARIAS
Statesman, Nobel Peace Laureate

Dr. A.T. ARIYARATNE
Buddhist spiritual leader

Maurice BÉJART
Dancer/Choreographer

Prof. Thomas BERRY
Theologian/Scientist

Sir Arthur C. CLARKE
Writer

H.H. The XIVth DALAI LAMA
Statesman/Spiritual leader

Dr. Riane EISLER
Feminist Historian/Activist

Milos FORMAN
Film Director

Peter GABRIEL
Musician

Dr. Jane GOODALL
Scientist

Rivka GOLANI
Musician

H.E. Mikhail GORBACHEV
Opinion Leader/Statesman

H.E. Arpád GÖNCZ
Writer/Statesman

Prof. Otto Herbert HAJEK
Sculptor

H.E. Václav HAVEL
Writer/Statesman

Pir Vilayat INAYAT-KHAN
Sufi Spiritual Leader

Miklós JANCSÓ
Film Director

Ken-Ichiro KOBAYASHI
Orchestra Director

Gidon KREMER
Musician

Prof. Hans KÜNG
Theologian/Christian Spiritual Leader

Prof. Shu-hsien LIU
Philosopher

Eva MARTON
Opera Singer

Zubin MEHTA
Orchestra Director

Dr. Edgar MITCHELL
Scientist/Astronaut

Prof. Edgar MORIN
Philosopher/Sociologist

Dr. Robert MULLER
Educator/Activist

Ute-Henriette OHOVEN
UNESCO Ambassador

Prof. Gillo PONTECORVO
Film Director

Mary ROBINSON
Political and Human Rights Leader

Mstislav ROSTROPOVICH
Orchestra Director

Sir Josef ROTBLAT
Scientist/Nobel Peace Laureate

Dr. Peter RUSSELL
Philosopher/Futurist

Masami SAIONJI
Japanese Spiritual Leader

H.E. Karan SINGH
Hindu Spiritual Leader

Sir Sigmund STERNBERG
Interfaith Spiritual Leader

His Grace Desmond TUTU
Spiritual Leader, Archbishop

Liv ULLMANN
Film Actor/Director

Sir Peter USTINOV
Actor/Writer/Director

H.E. Vigdis FINNBOGADOTTIR
Political Leader

H.E. Richard von WEIZSÄCKER
Statesman

Prof. Elie WIESEL
Writer/Nobel Peace Laureate

Betty WILLIAMS
Activist/Nobel Peace Laureate

Prof. Mohammed YUNUS
Economist/Financial Leader

Introduction

Mikhail Gorbachev

Dear Reader – this Action Handbook for the 21st Century speaks to you in person. Indeed, this is a message that is addressed to you and to all of us. It is written in the hope that you will not only read it, but will also think through the things it tells you. Furthermore that you will draw the necessary conclusions, your own conclusions, for yourself, your family, your friends, and everyone close to you.

Why did the author of this book, Ervin Laszlo – the famous scientist, humanist and president of the Club of Budapest – choose this specific form, the form of a message addressed to us, to each and every one of us, his readers?

In general, when someone's future or some aspect of the world that surrounds us in daily life is in question, we see the gist of the issue fairly easily and quickly. We see the advantages and dangers and draw the conclusions, deciding what steps to take. This is natural, it corresponds with our habits, it is part of our everyday thinking and behaviour. For someone living in a complex world, common sense dictates that he or she must think about whether or not to adapt to the given circumstances, or try to change them.

The situation is different when we confront problems that affect the whole of the world, the destiny of all humankind. We are not used to questions of such dimensions. It may seem that they are far away and that some time, somehow, they will be solved, indeed that someone up there is taking care of them. Why us? We are only little people.

This is why the book in your hand, dedicated to global, world-encompassing problems, addresses you in plain and logical language and marshals persuasive evidence. This makes our task easier. The task is simple. Get down to the basics, understand that global problems are not foreign to us. They are our problems. We are all touched by them, and touched by them not any less than we are by ordinary, everyday things. And it is we, each one of us, who not only can understand these problems, but can also do something significant to overcome them.

Just What is Really at Stake?

The fact is that with the passing of time a whole pyramid of diverse problems has been accumulating in every part of the world: social, political, economic and cultural problems. Contradictions have appeared in society – in a different way in each country, but present all the same – and they have created conflicts and crises, sometimes even wars. The relationship between man and nature has become more and more complex and strained. The air has become poisoned, rivers polluted, forests decimated. The number of contradictions keeps growing, and they are becoming deeper. Society is showing the symptoms of sickness.

In our various ways all of us, in every part of the world, have expressed our dissatisfaction with this state of affairs, have demanded changes, and are still demanding them. Isn't this story familiar? I think it is.

However, at a certain point these challenges and contradictions become so serious that changes become unavoidable. If the leaders who decide the life of society prove incapable of understanding the necessity for changes, and of doing something about it, people will not put up with them any longer. Violent movements will arise, strikes, and disturbances. Society will enter a period of crisis. How will the crisis be resolved? This is difficult to predict. Society's sickness affects every single member, every single citizen, and threatens everyone with suffering. The end result may be an explosion, a bloodbath that nobody wants, yet which comes about spontaneously.

Another Way Out

Is there another way out, a path beyond the crisis? The book in your hand gives an answer: yes, there is another way. We must not wait until society's crisis reaches the danger point. We must act! Every person can act. If everyone does his or her bit, together we can accomplish what is necessary. We can make an impact on those who decide the politics and the destiny of society, and motivate them to begin making the necessary changes. Changes that not only resolve the crisis, but take us on a path of survival, of healthy development for people and nature, and a better quality of life for all. That is our salvation.

The human community has reached the point where it must decide whether it allows events to take their course (and if it does, we will all be put to a difficult test) or whether it manages to make the turning that changes the character and the content of development for the benefit of humankind. To make this decision, we must first become conscious that a turning is truly necessary. Then we must understand what we must do to avoid the worst, and how we must do it.

This book helps us to understand the current situation of our planet and to find the path we must take. It helps us determine what we must do and how we must do it to ensure our common well-being. The future that confronts us is an open future. All of us – and that includes you, the reader – can do our bit to decide it.

Read this handbook, and start thinking. This is important for you, for your family, for your children and grandchildren, for your friends, and for everyone around you.

May 2002

1 The World in Your Hands

The world needs changing. It is not sustainable, and sooner or later it will change. Predicting which way it will change is not the challenge before us: the future is not to be foretold, it is to be created. The challenge is to create a positive future. And that is up to us – to you and to me.

We can create a more peaceful and sustainable world. We are not obliged to live forever in crisis and conflict. We can choose harmony, co-operation, liveable communities, and a value system that nourishes and sustains us in place of a world that is unsustainable economically, socially and ecologically.

When we take stock of current conditions we see that transformation is essential, and it is imminent. The degeneration of the local and global environment, the inequity of the globalised economic and social system, and the stress, misery, and resentment, which now exist among billions of people, has created an untenable situation. The September 11 terrorist attack on New York and Washington is not the cause of crisis in the world: it is one of its dramatic symptoms. The crisis we experience is the consequence of the way the world's economic and social system is structured and the way in which it operates.

The economic and social system of the world has brought unparalleled wealth to a few, and marginalisation and misery to many. It has concentrated production, trade, finance and communication, and has created national and regional unemployment, widening income gaps, and mounting environmental degradation. The benefits of economic growth, for long the main indicator of progress, have become ever more concentrated. While the richest 20% of the world population become richer still, the poorest 20% are pressed into abject poverty, barely surviving in shantytowns and urban ghettos.

These conditions are socially and politically explosive. They fuel resentment and revolt, and provoke massive migration from the countryside to the cities, and from the poorer to the richer regions. Fanatics wage holy wars and resort to terrorism, and organised crime engages in information fraud, corruption, and traffic in women and children as well as drugs, organs and weapons. As long as people harbour hate and the desire for revenge, they cannot co-exist peacefully and co-operatively. Whether the cause is the wounded ego of a person or the wounded self-respect of a people; whether it is the wish for personal revenge or a holy war in defence of a faith, the potential for violence remains. Attaining peace in people's hearts is a precondition of attaining peace in the world. And inner peace depends very much on creating more equitable conditions in the global village into which we have precipitated ourselves.

The global village is full of problems. In industrialised countries, job security is a thing of the past. In poor countries, poverty is aggravated by hunger, joblessness and degrading conditions. Both rich and poor countries overwork productive lands, contaminate rivers, lakes and seas, and draw down water tables. And the gap between the modern and the traditional segments of society rends apart the structures and institutions on which social stability depend.

Investment flows mostly between rich countries, where it has the best chances of generating high and quick returns. Although some $19 trillion is invested in the world's stock markets, only 1% of direct foreign investment reaches the poorest 20% of the world's population.

The world's economy is not only inequitable: because of the workings of the international monetary system it is inherently unsustainable. Most of the money in the world is supplied as loans by the banking system and has to be repaid with interest. Servicing the ever-increasing debt requires continual growth in the economy, and on our finite planet endless quantitative growth encounters natural limits. Moreover, the present system encourages financial speculation on a colossal scale with over $1 trillion moving around the globe every day in search of short-term gain. This money is not financing trade or production; it is merely gambling on market dynamics and currency fluctuation – hence the term the global casino.

Reforming the way the world's economy is financed is urgent and necessary. It calls for a new sense of responsibility, for behaviour suited to life in a tightly interdependent global village, where the actions of each affect the destiny of all. Economic and financial competition needs to be tempered with greater co-operation and fairness, and production as well as consumption must become more attuned to social and ecological considerations. This would enhance the sustainability of the contemporary world by creating more economic justice and reducing the level of conflict.

Unsustainability in our global village also has ecological roots. In the past, a functional equilibrium could be maintained between human settlements and the biosphere. The human exploitation of the environment was more modest. With primitive technologies and small populations the supply of natural resources seemed endless, and environmental damage insignificant. When improved technologies depleted or destroyed a local environment, there were other environments to conquer and exploit.

In the middle of the 19th century the world's population reached one billion, and its resource use increased dramatically. Both population and the use of resources continued to grow throughout the 20th century. In the past 50 years, our parents and grandparents used more natural resources than in all of the preceding millennia put together. Today the global village has more than 6 billion inhabitants. While our numbers are enormous, our bodies still constitute a tiny 0.014% of the planet's entire biomass, and a modest 0.44% of the biomass of all animals. The load we place on the environment is out of proportion to our numbers.

The 'ecological footprint' (the area of land required to support a settlement) gives a quantitative estimate of the human overload of nature. It defines the share of the planet's biological productivity used by an individual, a city, a nation, or all of humanity. If the footprint of a settlement is larger than its area, that settlement is not independently sustainable. A city is intrinsically unsustainable because very few of the natural resources used by its inhabitants come from within its boundaries. Most of them, such as food, water, and waste disposal, rely on hinterlands and catchments. But entire regions and countries could well be sustainable: their ecological footprint need not extend beyond their territories. This, however, is not the case. In a survey commissioned by the Earth Council of Costa Rica, the ecological footprints of 52 countries, the home of 80% of the world's peoples, were examined. Forty-two of these countries had footprints that exceeded their territory.

We can see the roots of the problem when we compare the footprint of individuals with the biological productivity of the planet. In 1996, the Earth's biosphere had 12.6 billion hectares of biologically productive space, making up about one quarter of the planetary surface. It comprised 9.4 billion hectares of land and 3.2 billion hectares of fishing ground. Equitably shared, in a population of 5.7 billion this yielded an earth-share of 2.18 hectares per person. Now that there are 6.3 billion, the biosphere's biological productivity remains at best constant. Thus today's earth-share is just 2.1 hectares for each man, woman and child on the planet. But in the 52 countries examined, the average footprint came to 2.8 hectares.

The World Wildlife Fund's Living Planet Report 2000 measured the footprints of 151 nations. The study included the largest, most highly populated countries, and gave a fair measure of the world situation. It appears that today humanity exceeds its Earth-share by nearly a third: 30.7%. The 75 countries that consume above their Earth-share make up 21% of humanity. Among them the United Arab Republic, Singapore, and the United States exceed their share nearly twelve times (in the U.S. the average footprint is 12.5 hectares, which is 31 acres). Even if the per capita footprint in the poorest countries, such as Bangladesh, is only 0.5 hectares, our species still lives beyond its means: it exceeds the capacity of the planet to produce food, water and wood, absorb pollution, and provide habitable space for all people.

The situation would be worse still if all countries were to adopt development on the Western model. If the footprint of the 42 rich countries were to be attained by all of the 189 formally constituted nation-states of the world, the global excess would be 100%. To remain in balance with our ecological base, we would require another planet the size of Earth.

Humanity not only overloads nature, it also impairs it. The progressive degradation of the environment was not widely recognised until the 1980s. Prior to that, the success of technological civilisation had obscured the fact that the cycles of nature became progressively degraded. Chemically bolstered mechanised agriculture increased yields per acre and made more acres available for cultivation, but it also increased the growth of algae in our lakes and waterways. Chemicals such as DDT proved to be effective insecticides, but they poisoned entire animal, bird, and insect populations. We now produce 300 to 500 million tons of hazardous chemicals each year, and when some part of this reaches the environment it poisons people as well as plants and animals. In industrialised countries we have between 500 and 1,000 times more lead in our body than is good for us. And we have polluted lakes and rivers and drawn down water tables to the point where one in six in the human family lack clean drinking water and two in five do not have adequate sanitation.

We are approaching the outer edge of the Earth's capacity to sustain human life. The 2002 Living Planet report warned that humankind is plundering the planet at a pace that outstrips its capacity to support life. More than a third of the natural resources of the world has been destroyed by human activity over the past three decades, and if these trends continue, by the year 2050, to support the human population, we will need two other planets the size of Earth. The unsustainability of the world is aggravated by the fact that ecosystems do not collapse piecemeal. We have been operating on the assumption that in nature cause and effect is proportional, so that an additional ounce of pollution produces an additional ounce of damage. This, however, is not so. Ecosystems may be polluted for many years without any change at all, then flip into an entirely different condition. Gradual changes create cumulative vulnerability, until a single shock to the system, such as a flood or a drought, knocks the system into a different state, less adapted to sustaining human life and economic activity.

A leap into a catastrophic new state can also occur in the global climate. According to a recent report by the US National Academy of Sciences, abrupt changes can come about when the climate system is forced to cross some threshold. The global warming trend projected over the course of the next 100 years (a rise in temperatures somewhere between 1.4 and 5.8 degrees centigrade) could actually occur in the next few years. The new climate would undermine human settlements and ecologies throughout the world. Forests would be consumed by fires, grasslands would dry out and turn into dust bowls, wildlife would disappear and diseases, such as cholera, malaria and yellow fever, would decimate human populations.

Our global village is inequitable, and it is neither economically nor ecologically sustainable. This situation cannot be prolonged indefinitely. We either achieve a higher level of sustainability, or risk major havoc.

Half a century ago Albert Einstein noted that we cannot solve a problem with the same kind of thinking that gave rise to it. Today's Nobel scientists agree. A Declaration signed by one hundred Laureates at the conclusion of the Nobel Peace Prize Centennial Symposium in December of 2001 noted, "The most profound danger to world peace in the coming years will stem not from the irrational acts of states or individuals but from the legitimate demands of the world's dispossessed." They ended the Declaration saying, "To survive in the world we have transformed, we must learn to think in a new way".

New thinking, and the economic, social and ecological behaviour that follows it, are soft factors in the life of society, but when it comes to deciding our future they have more weight than hard factors such as money and power. Not heavy-handed intervention from the top down, but timely change percolating from the grass roots up can set the world on the road to peace and sustainability.

The bottom line is that the urgently required worldwide transformation calls for positive changes in the way you and others around you live and think. As Mikhail Gorbachev has made clear, when all is said and done, the future is in your hands. With new thinking and sustainable living, you can change the world.

2 Breakdown or Breakthrough

A Choice of Futures

There is not just one possible future before us, but many. In the final count we face a negative future of total breakdown, as well as a positive future of stupendous breakthrough. The initial conditions are the same for all scenarios.

- Increasing population pressure: 77 million humans added to the world population every year, 97% of them in the poor countries
- spreading poverty: nearly two billion living on less than two dollars a day, more than one billion at the lower limits of physical subsistence
- widening gap between rich and poor people as well as rich and poor economies: 80% of the human population is responsible for 14% of global consumption, while the richest 20% accounts for 86%
- growing threat of social breakdown and rise of mindless violence in countries rich and poor
- intolerance and fundamentalism: for example, in Afghanistan, Bosnia, Kashmir, Turkey and the Middle East, and worldwide through networks like Al Qaida

- food and water shortages, e.g. in sub-Saharan Africa, China, Southern Asia, Meso-America
- accelerating climate change: extremes of cold and heat, violent storms, changed rainfall patterns
- worsening industrial, urban, and agricultural pollution: changed chemical composition of the atmosphere, desalination and impoverishment of agricultural lands, lowering and poisoning of water tables
- accelerating deforestation and reduction of biodiversity: disappearance of tropical rainforests, loss of an untold number of species, monocultures on cultivated lands
- rising sea levels: loss of low-lying plains and river valleys in Southern Asia, flooding of island countries in the Pacific, threat to coastal cities throughout the world

The Breakdown Scenario

The First Signs
- growing incidence of harvest failure due to changing weather patterns
- starvation and unsanitary conditions accelerating the spread of HIV/AIDS and other epidemics
- wars over access to fresh water and staple food supply in Asia, Africa, and Latin America
- millions of climate refugees from flooded coastal cities and low-lying areas
- massive waves of destitute migrants moving toward North America and Europe

Subsequent Events

- breakdown of the world financial system reflected in the cancellation of global trade agreements and disruption of trade flows
- deepening insecurity and violence from maverick and organised terrorism
- international and intercultural conflict resulting in local and regional wars
- rise of strong-arm régimes in many parts of the world, especially in the hardest-hit regions of the South

The Outcome

- worldwide spread of terrorism, corruption, anarchy, and organised crime
- collapse of the North Atlantic alliance linking Europe and North America
- breakdown of relations between the US and Russia
- regional wars in the Middle East, South and Southeast Asia, Sub-Saharan Africa, and Latin America
- inclusion of nuclear, chemical, and biological weapons in regional wars
- global escalation of armed conflict

The Breakthrough Scenario

The First Signs

- Population pressures, poverty, fanaticism, and a variety of environmental threats and disasters trigger positive changes in the way people think. The idea that another world is possible captures the imagination of more and more people. As in England and Russia during World War II, and in America in the aftermath of

September 11, people in different societies and different walks of life pull together to confront the threat they face in common
- Non-governmental organisations link up through the Internet and develop shared strategies to restore local economies and local environments and promote socially and ecologically responsible policies in local and national government and business. A non-governmental World Futures Council is established at the same time as an electronic E-Parliament comes online to link parliamentarians worldwide and provide a forum for debates on the best ways to serve the common interest
- Governments and corporations begin to respond to calls for greater social and ecological responsibility from growing movements of civil society

The Next Developments

- Money is increasingly re-assigned from military and defence budgets to fund practical attempts at conflict resolution together with a worldwide programme to restore the Earth as the concept of an ecological economy is becoming widely accepted
- A movement to promote 'localisation' is gaining in strength, balancing the one-sided forms of globalisation through the efficient use of the human, natural and financial resources of local environments
- Reforms are undertaken in the world's monetary system. A world currency is put into circulation by the reformed World Bank Group on the basis of population size rather than financial power, creating a more equitable flow of money among the world's disparate economies; at the same time local currencies continue to grow and develop.

The Outcome

- A worldwide renewable energy programme is created, paving the way toward a new industrial revolution making use of solar and other renewable energy sources to transform the global economy and lift marginalised populations out of the vicious cycles of poverty
- Agriculture is restored to a place of primary importance in the economy, not only for the production of staple foods, but for growing energy crops and raw materials for diverse branches of manufacturing
- Governance structures are reformed so as to move toward a participatory Earth Democracy, releasing a surge of creative energy among people whose voice can now be heard
- As a result of such developments international and intercultural mistrust, ethnic conflict, racial oppression, economic injustice, and gender inequality give way to a more peaceful and sustainable world, based on a higher level of trust and co-operation among the world's many peoples, cultures, and economies. [1]

These two scenarios illustrate the outcomes that can follow from today's unsustainable situation. The difference between them is not in the initial conditions. The world from which they take off is the same: it is today's world. The difference is in the way people respond to conditions in this world. As Einstein knew, the decisive factor is not the problem, but the way we think about it. In today's world, new thinking can make a crucial difference. The shape of tomorrow will be decided by how we think and live today. Just as the legendary flap of the wings of a butterfly can create an air current that amplifies and amplifies until it changes the weather on the other side of the globe, in a condition of unsustainability, minor actions produce butterfly effects that change the system.

Two Ways of Thinking and Living

In the course of history people have thought in widely different ways about themselves and the world around them. There were different conceptions of society, life, and honour and dignity in the East and in the West, in classical epochs, in the Middle Ages, and in the Modern Age. Perhaps more remarkably, there are different ways of thinking even among people in modern industrial societies. This is highlighted by a recent survey of opinions and lifestyles in the US population, [2] which shows that a surprising number of Americans think and live in a new, more responsible way.

US Cultures

The mainstream culture of America is the culture of the moderns. Moderns are stalwart supporters of the consumer society, they share the rationality that shaped it and made the US into the largest economy in the world. Theirs is the culture of banks and stock exchanges and the office towers and factories of big business; theirs are the values taught in the establishment schools and colleges. In 1999, this was the culture of 48% of the American people, some 93 million out of about 193 million adults, more men than women. Family income was in the region of $40,000 to $50,000 per year, situating moderns in the upper-middle income bracket.

While the moderns are still dominant in the US, another

culture is growing rapidly. This is the culture of the creatives. [3]
In 1999, cultural creatives had a 23.4% share of the US adult
population, counting almost twice as many women as men, with
the majority coming from the middle or the affluent classes.

People in these contrasting cultures think in vastly different
ways, and their thinking gives rise to vastly different ways of living.

The Moderns

Moderns share many of the traditional virtues and values of
Americans. They believe in God, in being honest, in the
importance of family and education, and in a fair day's pay for a
fair day's work. But some of their values and beliefs are less
conducive to a positive future. The principle aspirations of
moderns include:

- Making or having a lot of money
- Climbing the ladder of success with measurable steps
- Looking good
- Being on top of the latest trends
- Being entertained by the media

For the most part, moderns are convinced that:

- the body is much like a machine
- organisations, too, are much like machines
- either big business or big government is in control, and knows best
- bigger is better
- what can be measured is what gets done
- analysing things into their parts is the best way to solve a problem
- efficiency and speed are the top priorities – time is money
- life can be compartmentalised into separate spheres: work,

family, socialising, making love, education, politics, and religion
- being concerned with spirituality and the inner dimensions of life is flaky and immaterial to the real business of living

The Cultural Creatives

The cultural creatives espouse a different set of values and beliefs and adopt correspondingly different lifestyles.
- cultural creatives buy more books and magazines than moderns, listen to more radio, preferably news and classical music, and watch less television
- they are aggressive consumers of the arts and culture, more likely to go out and get involved, whether as amateurs or professionals
- creatives want the whole story of whatever they get in their hands, from cereal boxes to magazine articles. They dislike superficial advertising and product description, wanting to know how things originated, how they were made, who made them, and what will happen to them when they are discarded
- cultural creatives want real goods and services. They have led the consumer rebellion against products considered fake, imitation, throwaway, cliché, or merely fashionable
- cultural creatives do not buy on impulse but research what they consume, reading labels and assuring themselves that they are getting what they want. They do not simply buy the latest gadgets and innovations on the market. Many of them are only just getting on the Internet
- cultural creatives are consumers of intense, enlightening, or enlivening experience such as weekend workshops, spiritual

gatherings, personal growth events, and experiential vacations. With regard to material products, creatives prefer ecologically sound, efficient goods which can be repaired, and fuel efficient cars that can be recycled

- cultural creatives want their homes to be as ecologically balanced as possible. They avoid status displays and like to create a nest with interesting nooks and niches. Cultural creatives often like to work at home

- the common thread among cultural creatives is holism. This is shown in their preference for natural whole foods, holistic health care, whole system information, and holistic balance between work and play and consumption, and inner growth. They view themselves as synthesisers and healers, not just on the personal level but also in the community, at national and even global level. They aspire to create change in personal values and public behaviour that could shift the dominant culture beyond the fragmented and mechanistic world of the moderns.

In the United States the population of cultural creatives is growing. It numbered five million in 1965; today it numbers 50 million. A similar culture is growing in other parts of the world. A survey by the European Union's monthly Euro-Barometer questioned people in 15 of the Union's member states regarding their cultural and lifestyle preferences, and found that cultures similar to that of the cultural creatives are present in Europe in much the same proportion as in the US. [4]

These are hopeful developments. People who belong to the new cultures place less pressure on the environment and are more open to understanding others and co-operating with them. Their lifestyles are simpler, not for lack of money, but because of an intrinsic preference for simplicity and authenticity. More creatives than moderns could live on the planet without triggering religious and cultural conflicts, resource shortages, and ecological degradation.

NOTES

1. Readers can follow the unfolding of the breakthrough scenario to the year 2020 in the Postscript.

2. See Paul H. Ray and Sherry Ruth Anderson, *The Cultural Creatives* (Harmony Books, New York, 2000).

3. The third culture identified in this survey was that of the Traditionals. Members of this culture had family incomes in the relatively low range of $20,000 to $30,000 per year, due among other things to the reduced income of the many retirees among them. Traditionals are less relevant to the choice of futures before us than the other cultures. The mainly backward looking ideals of older people are not being taken up by the younger generation, and this population is dwindling.

4. More definite figures will be established by the Survey of Planetary Consciousness of the Club of Budapest, carried out in Germany, Italy, France, as well as Poland and Hungary. A further survey is projected for Japan. See the Club of Budapest's international website: club-of-budapest.org

3 New Ways to Think

Better ways of thinking are spreading in the world, but it is by no means certain that they will spread fast enough. If we are to increase our chances of moving towards a positive future, we must make sure that we think in a new and appropriate way. Let us begin by examining our beliefs.

Beliefs

We all hold beliefs, whether consciously or not. And some of our cherished beliefs have become obsolete. They no longer measure up to conditions in the world. Ask yourself: do I still maintain them? Here is a checklist:

- We are all separate individuals enclosed by our skin; if we co-operate it is only to promote our own interests.
- There is only one country and one people to whom I owe allegiance; all others are foreigners of no concern to me.
- Women's place is in the home; in the workplace women are best at assisting men, keeping order or cleaning up.
- The value of everything, including human beings, can be

calculated in money. What every economy needs is growth, and what every person wants is to get rich.

- Newer is always better. It is desirable and necessary, to buy and use the latest products and technologies. They make the economy grow and then everybody is better off.
- The future is none of my business. Why should I worry about the next generation? Every generation, like every person, has to look after itself.
- Crisis in the world is reversible. The economic, social, and ecological problems we are experiencing are temporary interludes, after which everything will get back to normal. Business as unusual has evolved out of business as usual, and will sooner or later reverse back into it.

A moment's reflection will tell us that such beliefs are obsolete. Seeing ourselves as individuals, separate and distinct from the social and the natural world in which we live, converts our natural impulse to seek our advantage into a short-sighted struggle among ever more unequal competitors. In today's inequitable yet interdependent world, engaging in this kind of struggle is not only unfair but is a threat to both winners and losers.

Believing that we owe allegiance to one country and one people only is a narrow form of patriotism. In fact we belong to many spheres and communities at the same time: we belong to a village or town, a culture or ethnic group, a business or industry, as well as to a nation. Some of these groups and communities are part of our country, others extend beyond it. In some parts of the world there are regional groups such as the European Union that also claim people's allegiance. And we all belong to the emerging global community. Ignoring our multiple ties in this interlinked world in favour of a single allegiance reduces the richness of our sphere of participation and suppresses our wider identities.

Relegating women to secondary tasks at work is part of a dangerously unbalanced perception. It ignores women's enormous and essential capacity for seeing things in context, and for championing so-called soft factors such as values, ethics, caring, and sustainability. These are crucial components of success in our unstable and crisis-prone world.

The reduction of everything and everybody to economic value may have made sense when the rapid growth of the economy pushed everything else into the background. It is obsolete in today's world, where more and more people are adopting non-material values, simpler lifestyles, and more modest forms of consumption.

Worshipping novelty is based on the mistaken belief that whatever is newer, consumes more energy and materials and is more expensive, must be better. This belief leads to a plethora of unnecessary services and wasteful goods, some of which can even make life more complicated, stressful and unhealthy.

Living without conscious concern about the future made sense in periods of stability and growth, when it seemed that every generation could ensure a good life for itself, but it is irresponsible in a world in which our lifestyle and consumption choices and professional and civic behaviour have a major, and perhaps irreversible, impact on the conditions we bequeath to our children.

Lastly, the belief that nothing changes fundamentally constrains creativity and makes us unable to learn from living in a world that is in rapid transformation.

Five Dangerous Beliefs

1 Nature Is Inexhaustible

The belief that nature is a limitless resource, and provides an infinite sink for waste, goes back thousands of years. It did not occur to the people of ancient Babylon, Sumer, Egypt, India and China that their environment could ever cease to supply them with edible plants, domestic animals, clean water and breathable air, or be fouled by waste and garbage. Nature seemed far too vast to be tainted, polluted, or defiled by human activity.

The classical belief in the inexhaustibility of nature was understandable and relatively innocuous. In most parts of the world people did not overstep the limits of nature's capacity to regenerate the required resources. They lived in balance with their environment. This changed about 10,000 years ago in the Fertile Crescent, now the Middle East. Here, at the cradle of Western civilisation, people were not content to live within the rhythms and cycles of nature but sought ways to harness the forces of their environment. In some places, such as ancient Sumer, their practices had vexing consequences. In deforested lands flash floods washed away irrigation channels and dams and left fields arid. In the course of millennia of cultivation, the Fertile Crescent of biblical times became an arid region dominated by sandy desert.

In classical times people could move on, colonising new lands and exploiting fresh resources. Today there is nowhere left to go. In a globally extended industrial civilisation wielding powerful technologies, believing in the inexhaustibility of nature is extremely dangerous. It gives rein to the over-use and thoughtless impairment of nature's resources, and to the overload of its self-regenerative cycles. If unchecked it will render nature incapable of satisfying the basic needs of our vast and still growing populations.

2 Life Is a Struggle for Survival

This age-old belief was given fresh substance by Darwin's theory of evolution through natural selection. The social application of Darwin's theory, 'Social Darwinism', holds that in society, as in nature, the fittest survive. This means that if we want to survive we have to be fit for the existential struggle – fitter than our competitors. In society fitness is not determined by genes. It is a personal and cultural trait, expressed as smartness, daring, ambition, and the ability to garner money and put it to work.

In the 1930s and 40s Social Darwinism was an inspiration of the Nazi ideology. It justified the conquest of foreign territories in the name of creating Lebensraum (living space) for Germany, and was put forward as a justification of the genocide of Jews, Slavs and Gypsies: the fitness – defined as the racial purity – of the Aryan race was to be preserved. In our day the consequences of Social Darwinism go beyond genocide and armed aggression to the subtler but similarly merciless struggle in the marketplace. In this struggle, fitness rewards corporate executives, international financiers, and speculators: they become rich and powerful. The gap between rich and poor produces frustration and ultimately violence. These consequences are conveniently ignored. The economic variant of Social Darwinism is nearly as dangerous as its military variant.

3 The Market Distributes Benefits

In the industrialised world, this obsolete belief elevates the market almost to the status of a tribal god. Our leadership accepts pollution and global warming as the unavoidable cost of market competition. Our economies sacrifice to it farmers and farmlands, forests, wetlands and prairies, ecosystems and watersheds. After all, the market distributes the benefits, so if one individual or one economy does well, the others will do well, too.

Unfortunately this belief leaves out of account a fact noted by economists themselves: the market distributes benefits only under conditions of near-perfect competition, where the playing field is level and all players have more or less the same number of chips. But in today's world the field is far from level and the chips are far from being evenly distributed. Consequently the global market favours the rich at the expense of the poor. The richest 20% of humankind earn 90 times more than the poorest 20%.

4 The Richer You Are the Better You Are

This modern belief justifies the struggle for profit and wealth. It suggests that there is equivalence between the size of one's wallet – as demonstrated among other things by the size of one's car and one's house – and the personal worth of the owner of the wallet.

This equation of human worth with financial worth has been consciously fuelled by business. In former years, companies advertised conspicuous consumption as the ideal. Writing in 1950s America, Victor Lebov, a retailing analyst declared, "Our enormously productive economy demands that we make consumption our way of life, that we convert the buying and use of goods into rituals, that we seek our spiritual satisfaction, our ego satisfaction, in consumption. The economy needs things consumed, burned, worn out, replaced, and discarded at an ever-increasing rate." [5]

Today we know that the classical forms of consumerism lead to over-consumption and resource-depletion, and are neither healthy nor sustainable. The quantitative forms of economic growth are not inherently desirable. The seemingly limitless accumulation of wealth in a nation's economy, as with the single-minded pursuit of wealth in an individual, is a sign of immaturity and insecurity, rather than of character and strength. The belief that the richer you are, the better you are, is ripe for the dustheap.

5 The Way to Peace is Through War

The ancient Romans had a saying: if you aspire to peace, prepare for war. This matched their conditions and experience. The Romans had a worldwide empire, containing rebellious races and cultures, and with barbarian tribes at its periphery. Maintaining this empire required a constant exercise of military power. Today the nature of power is very different, but the belief about war is much the same. Like Rome in classical times, the US is a global power, but one which is economic rather than political. Maintaining it requires not armed enforcement but fair and sustainable relations between the world's remaining superpower and the rest of the international community.

Inserting armed forces in a conflict has become a questionable strategy. Military might can still produce victory, but it is unlikely to produce peace. Any state or group can buy hi-tech weapons and can use them in guerrilla warfare and terrorism. The principle of an eye for an eye and a tooth for a tooth makes all parties blind and toothless.

War is also highly wasteful of financial resources. World military expenditure is about $2 billion per day – a mind-boggling sum that could be far better spent. A 1998 report of the

United Nations Development Programme estimated that an expenditure of about $40 billion per year, if maintained for 10 years, could ensure that everyone in the world has access to an adequate diet, safe water, basic health care, and proper sanitation.

The many lesser and the five particularly dangerous beliefs give us a faulty concept of man and nature. They tell us that our responsibilities end with satisfying our needs and the demands of our economy, that other people are none of our business, and that we can do as we please with the environment. They blind us to our responsibilities towards the wider human community, and towards the planet's biosphere, our life-sustaining environment.

Rights

The universal rights proclaimed in the 20th century are significant milestones in the international community's striving for fairness and justice. They are contained within the International Covenant on Civil and Political Rights, and the International Covenant on Economic, Social and Cultural Rights. So far, these covenants have not achieved their objectives. The rights are universal, but the respect accorded to them is not.

Some of the rights adopted by the international community are difficult and costly to implement. However the civil and political rights – the right to vote, the right not to be tortured, and the right to free speech – do not come into this category. These are essentially negative liberties: freedoms from discrimination, oppression and arbitrary constraint. They call for doing away with dictatorial and repressive practices; they require mainly acts of omission within the scope of democratic states.

By contrast, the second set of rights – economic, social and cultural rights that include the right to health, the right to food and the right to employment – call for positive liberties: these are freedoms to lead a life of sanity, dignity, and well-being. They call for acts of commission which are often costly and difficult to carry out. Democratic governments by themselves do not have the means and the power to ensure all of the positive liberties for all of their people; they require the co-operation of civil society, especially the private sector of commerce, finance, and industry.

Even a cursory review of conditions in the world shows that some of the negative liberties are quite well respected. In most parts of the world people can vote, and express themselves without overt censorship. Torture is confined to a few remaining repressive régimes. Positive liberties, on the other hand, are widely neglected. With the exception of a few relatively small and prosperous countries – among them the European Nordic countries – the joint action required for implementing these rights is as yet missing. Yet respecting the right of each human being to food, shelter, education, and gainful work is a precondition of ensuring a positive future for all people. The 20th century may enter history as the Century of Rights (and perhaps also as a century of wars and destruction), but the 21st century must become a Century of Responsibilities if it is to become a century of peace – or any kind of century in the life of humankind at all.

Ethics

In critical times, ethics are of decisive importance. Beliefs orient our thinking, but ethics decide what we do.

Unless we are deeply religious, spiritually inclined or philosophically versed, we are far less aware of our ethics than of our beliefs. We should rectify this. We should ask, are the ethics that we hold right for today's world? Are the things we judge good, truly good and worth striving for?

What we hold right and good cannot be dictated from above by anyone, be it parent, priest, teacher, boss, or political leader. We must decide our ethics for ourselves. In a democratic society a wide variety of opinions can be held and a great many goals pursued. But there is a limit on our freedom to define our ethics: what we hold right and good must mesh with what is right and good for the communities in which we live. Today we live not only in a local community – a village, town or city. We live not only in one state and nation, and not even in just one region and culture. We live in an interacting and interdependent global village. Our ethics must also mesh with what is right and good for humanity.

But with some notable exceptions, the global dimension is still missing in people's ethics. This is evident in the way most people live, or aspire to live. As we have seen, when multiplied by the number of people in the world, the ecological footprint of individuals is larger than the total ecology of the planet. Individual lifestyles have become globally unsustainable.

Without a global dimension to our ethics we face difficult times. A statement signed by 1,670 scientists from 70 countries made this point. "A great change in our stewardship of the Earth and the life on it is required if vast human misery is to be avoided and our global home on this planet is not to be irretrievably mutilated."[6]   The scientists, including 102 Nobel laureates, concluded that a global ethic must motivate a great movement, to convince reluctant leaders and governments, and reluctant peoples, to effect the needed changes.

A global or planetary ethic is not partisan, serving one country or culture above others. The basic principle is treat others as you expect others to treat you. This is a universal 'golden rule' expressed in all the great religions of humankind. In Christianity it was pronounced by Jesus: "In everything, do unto others as you would have them do unto you." In Judaism the golden rule is expressed in the Talmud: "What is hateful to you, do not do to your neighbour" and in Islam it is present in Mohammed's tenet, "Not one of you truly believes until you wish for others that which you wish for yourself." Hinduism says, "This is the sum of duty: do not do to others what would cause pain if done to you," and the Baha'i writings tell us that "If thine eyes be turned towards justice, choose thou for thy neighbour that which thou choosest for thyself." The Buddha advised, "Treat not others in ways that you yourself would find hurtful" and Confucius said: "Do not do to others what you do not want done to yourself". [7]

In the tradition, 'you' has stood for neighbour, friend, and fellow member of the local community. That was the range within which people interacted. Today the range of human interaction is global: what any of us does affects all others. Our ethics must expand as well. What any member of the global community does must not be injurious to any other member of this community.

We are far from attaining this goal. What some people do is injurious to the rest of the global community, even if they do not do it on purpose. The rich use up an inordinate share of the planet's resources and produce the lion's share of its waste and pollution, and the poor are forced to over exploit the lands, waters and forests that surround their habitations. If these practices continue we shall soon be missing essential resources and live in an impoverished and dramatically unhealthy environment.

The lesson is clear: if we do not want others to violate our right to a healthy environment and to a fair share of the planet's resources, we must not degrade other people's environment and interfere with their access to basic resources. In today's world, "Do as you would be done by" becomes "Live in a way that permits all people on the planet to live".

Adopting this planetary ethic does not mean that we must live in poverty, or even with extreme frugality. All people do not need to live in the same way we do; they may not even want to do so. The goal is not uniformity but fairness. We can aim for fairness and justice in the world without depriving ourselves of the pleasures and enjoyment of a reasonable and responsible life. We can strive for personal excellence, growth, and enjoyment, even for comfort and non-wasteful luxury. We must simply define the pleasures and achievements of life in relation to the quality of enjoyment and level of satisfaction they provide, rather than in terms of the amount of money they cost and the quantity of materials and energy they require. Then we give a fair chance to all people in the world to live a life of basic dignity and well-being.

Notes

5] Quoted by Alan Durning in How Much is Enough? (Norton, 1992).

6] Statement of the Union of Concerned Scientists, 1993.

7] Sources for the Golden Rule citations:

Christianity, Matthew 7:12;

Judaism, Hillel, Talmud, Shibbath 31a;

Islam, The Prophet Muhammad, Hadith;

Hinduism, Mahabharata 5:1517

Buddhism, The Buddha, Udana-Varga 5.18;

Zoroastrianism, Shayast-Na-Shayast 13.29;

Confucianism, Confucius, Analects 15.23.

4 Sustainable Ways to Live

Updating our beliefs, respecting universal rights, and adopting planetary ethics are new ways to think. Practical things follow: new, more sustainable ways you and I can live.

Things You Can Do Now

Some of the things we need to do can stand no delay. If you want to choose a path of sustainability and peace instead of escalating conflict and crisis, you must change the way you live. Here is a list of things to do in your private life, in the world of business, and in the civic sphere.

Things you can do in your private life

Nobody is an island. How we live and what we do affects others around us. In an interdependent and interacting world, each of us is a factor in the future of all. Some aspects of our private lives have become public business.

The principle governing responsible action is ageless. Doing good and doing well are not contradictory: they go together. If you live and act in a way that is good for others and for nature, you live and act in a way that is good for you as well.

The ten commandments of sustainable living are simple.

1 Live in a way that satisfies your essential needs without detracting from the chances of other people to satisfy theirs.

2 Live in a way that respects the right to life and development of all people, wherever they live, and whatever their ethnic origin, sex, citizenship and belief system.

3 Live in a way that safeguards the right to life and a healthy environment of all the things that live and grow on this Earth.

4 Pursue happiness, freedom, and personal fulfilment in consideration of the similar pursuits of your fellows in your community, country and culture and in the global community of all peoples, cultures and countries.

5 Do your best to help those less privileged than you to live without hunger and penury, whether they live next door or in another part of the world.

6 Join with like-minded people to preserve or restore the integrity of the environment so it can generate and regenerate the resources essential for human life and well-being.

7 Help children and young people to discover sustainable ways of living and acting.

8 Ask your government to beat swords into ploughshares and

deal peacefully and co-operatively with other nations and cultures recognising the legitimate aspirations for a better life and a life-supporting environment of all the peoples, cultures and countries of the world.

9 Patronise businesses that produce goods and offer services that satisfy your needs and the needs of other people without impairing the environment and aggravating the gap between rich and poor in your community and the world.

10 Give preference to newspapers and magazines, television and radio programmes and Internet sites that provide regular and reliable information on the trends and events that affect your life, and help you and others in your community take informed decisions on crucial issues.

Sustainable lifestyle choices need to be made:
* when choosing products for yourself, instead of throw-away items that use a great deal of energy and raw material, give preferences to functional devices that are made to last, are locally produced, and do the job with minimum waste of energy and materials
* when choosing your work or profession, rather than striving to amass the most money in the shortest time, engage in an activity that is useful and beneficial to community and country, and does not harm humans and nature
* when selecting your home furnishings, instead of looking for items that make the neighbours see how much you can afford, choose natural materials that last and make for warmth and sociability in your home

- when choosing your clothes, avoid unhealthy synthetic material and rather than looking for conspicuous and ostentatious labels, strive to express your personality and the values of your culture and community
- and when deciding your daily diet, rather than choosing unhealthy and carelessly produced junk foods, choose organically and where possible, locally grown products that provide healthy nourishment and do not despoil the environment.

Such choices have a major and generally unsuspected impact on humanity's well-being in the world. An estimated twenty million people die of malnutrition and starvation every year, yet one hundred million people could be sustained by the land, water, and energy saved if Americans ate 10% less meat. It takes 25 gallons of water to produce one pound of wheat, but 5,214 gallons of water plus 16 pounds of grain and soy to produce one pound of beef.

These things are not difficult to do, and they do not call for major sacrifices. On the contrary, they bring many benefits. You become a better neighbour and friend, and you will live more healthily – by eating less meat, for example, you drastically reduce your chances of major heart attack. And you will have the satisfaction of knowing that you are doing your best to be a responsible member of your community, your country, and the whole human family.

Things you can do in the world of business

The things you can do in the world of business are just as important as those in your private life. The business companies that design and produce today's plethora of goods and services and the technologies and infrastructures required, wield unprecedented power and have unprecedented wealth. The world's top five hundred industrial corporations employ only 0.05% of the human population but control 70% of world trade, 80% of direct foreign investment, and 25% of world economic output. The sales of the largest companies, such as General Motors, Ford, Mitsui, Mitsubishi, Royal Dutch Shell, Exxon and Wal-Mart, exceed the GDP of dozens of countries, including Poland and Norway, Greece, Thailand, and Israel. Global corporations have become a major factor in choosing our future.

Wielding power and wealth entails responsibility. Industrial companies have been a major force in the destruction of the environment, and major companies in all fields have contributed to the unequal distribution of wealth in the world. It is time that business leaders accept that power entails responsibility. Responsible management requires that managers switch from a shareholder philosophy to a stakeholder philosophy. It is up to you and me, their clients and customers, to insist that they make this switch.

The shareholder philosophy was put forward by Milton Friedman in an influential 1970 article in The New York Times Magazine. In this model, management is merely the agent of the company's owners, and its sole responsibility is to represent their interests – which means making profit for the shareholders. The concept of stakeholders was not widely known at the time. It grew to prominence later, when it became evident that corporations are a decisive factor in the life of the communities and countries where they operate. In the current concept, the company's stakeholders include not only the shareholders but also employees, partners, clients and consumers, and the people of the communities where they operate.

You can promote the shift to a stakeholder philosophy by patronising companies that embrace it, and boycotting or ignoring those that persist in the obsolete concept that the responsibility of a business begins and ends with the short-term profit of its shareholders. As a client and customer, as a shareholder, and as a member of the community where the company operates, you can insist that management:

- accurately and honestly represents to the public the long-term benefits and costs of the company's products and services, including their safety, durability, social consequences, environmental toxicity, reusability and recyclability
- gives preference to ethical companies as partners and associates, and refuses to do business with companies that behave unfairly toward their employees, customers and the communities, or degrade the environment
- actively seeks to reduce pollution and environmental damage and minimise waste in the company's production processes, and throughout its supply and distribution chain
- consults its employees when formulating the goals and objectives of the enterprise
- takes an active interest in the lives of employees, discovering their concerns, understanding their needs, and contributing to their personal development
- takes a similarly active interest in the people and the concerns of the local communities, encouraging employees to devote part of their time to social work or the protection of the environment. [8]

As a concerned citizen you can also join with friends to buy a minimum number of shares in a company – or simply join one of the many newly arising shareholders associations – and raise your voice and use your vote. This is an effective way to request executives to provide full and honest accounts of corporate activities and the nature of corporate products and services, and to pay more attention to their company's attitude toward stakeholders and the environment.

Insisting that a company adopt a stakeholder philosophy serves its best interests. A more responsible attitude toward society and nature is becoming increasingly valued by the public. A survey of more than 1,000 US consumers in March 2001 and again in October, 2001, reported in the Harvard Business Review of March, 2002, showed a large increase in the importance people place on a company's behaviour in regard to the well-being of society. The question posed in the survey was, "I place importance on a company's support of charitable causes when I decide..."

what to buy or where to shop?

    pre-September 11:   52%

    post-September 11:   77%

where to work?

    pre-September 11:   48%

    post-September 11:   76%

which companies to invest in?

    pre-September 11:   40%

    post-September 11:   63%

which companies I would like to see doing business in my community?

    pre-September 11:   58%

    post-September 11:   80%

Responsibility for society and the environment is not mere charity, it is becoming a major factor of success in business. It is not just coincidence that the most publicised bankruptcies of recent times – Enron and K-Mart – involved companies that entirely lacked stakeholder responsibility. Enron was notorious for its greed and focus on short-term profit, and K-Mart came last on the Total Social Impact Foundation's ranking of the Standard & Poor 500 companies. Arthur Andersen and World.com were likewise noted for irresponsible and unethical practices. On the other hand many of the companies that came high on the list of 100 best Corporate Citizens turned out to be also successful in the market place.

There are more things we can do when it comes to the flow of information in our environment. The task is not to amplify this flow, for it is already enormous, but to make it relevant to our future. The information that reaches the public is largely determined by the market. The public gets what it is willing to buy. Believing that the public is interested in few things other than war, crime, sports, the stock market and the doings of the famous and the powerful, the major national and international media concentrate on sensational items with news value. But a daily diet of such items does not help people to make informed choices regarding crucial issues. There are more responsible ways the media could operate.

You can have an important role here, too: you can influence the strategies and values of the media by voicing your preferences and acting on them. You can select offerings that provide pertinent and positive news, rather than just sensational or negative items. A number of alternative good news reports and newsletters are published by private non-governmental organisations. There is also a full-sized newspaper devoted to these issues, Positive News, published in England. But such publications are only now beginning to reach a critical mass in society. Why not have a page or at least a column in the national daily papers devoted to positive news – or an entire weekend supplement? Why not daily or weekly programmes on radio and television, and well-structured sites on the Internet? Such offerings would render an important service. They would inform people about learning communities, ethical movements, ideas for responsible living, efficient, environmentally friendly technologies, and non-polluting products.

Asking for such news items to come on stream is not asking the media for charity. It is asking that they remain relevant to the concerns of the public, which, after all, is in their own best interest.

Things You Can Do in the Civic Sphere

Although business is more powerful than ever, in insecure times the role of government gains in importance. There are problems of public security and social well-being to which only an enlightened leadership can respond. If your government is not sufficiently enlightened, you should lift your voice, join with others and challenge the prevailing policy.

An enlightened leadership follows positive movements among its own people and encourages their unfolding. It seeks ways to place dialogue with other people aimed at understanding and accommodation above seeking purely economic advantages and political or military domination. As a concerned citizen you can request that your government:

- takes into account the changing lifestyles, patterns of consumption, values and expectations in the various cultures and subcultures of our society

- adopts safer and more efficient technologies in public services, especially in the energy, transport and communication sectors
- researches, designs and implements projects for healthier and more natural living in cities and towns
- offers a choice of up-to-date alternative healing methods in public health care
- makes available ways and means for people to enjoy the natural environment without destroying ecological balances and despoiling or reducing wilderness areas
- relates to other governments in a spirit of fairness and collaboration, making full use of the available institutions and channels for intergovernmental and international co-operation in the interest of peace and sustainability.

The responsibilities of government also include public education. The educational system can play an important role: it can follow up changes in values and beliefs in society, and insert a planetary dimension in discussions about ethics, rights, and responsibilities. It can enable children and young people to make wise and responsible choices on issues that decide their future. With more relevant information they grow up with more appropriate values, having only the children they truly want and raising them to become responsible citizens of their country and of the whole global community.

Notes

8. A more complete listing of responsibilities is given at the website of the Innov-Ethics Group, a business ethics consulting firm partnering the Club of Budapest: www.innov-ethics.com

5 Getting Started

Even a journey of a thousand miles begins with the first step, a Chinese proverb tells us. The journey before us is measured not in miles but in years, and we are not alone in setting out on it: we are joined by more than six billion fellow human beings. It is a crucial journey, taking us either to a more peaceful and sustainable world or to conflict, violence, and chaos. We have to choose our path.

When Harry Truman said, "The buck stops here" he meant the desk of the president. Today the buck is more democratic: it stops with each and every one of us. You and I make the crucial difference between breakdown and breakthrough.

Choosing to grow up calls for new ways of thinking and living. It calls for re-examining our beliefs, respecting basic rights, and updating our ethics. It calls for informed behaviour as private individuals, as participants in the world of business, and as citizens of our country. Neither wealth and power, nor the control of territory and technology, make the crucial difference. How we think and how we live decides our destiny.

In the past most people thought that changing the world called for dominating other peoples and cultures and engineering nature, using military power, money, and technology. Today, changing the world calls for cultivating a more precious resource: our consciousness. Addressing a joint session of the US Congress, the Czech writer and president Václav Havel warned, "Without a global revolution in the sphere of human consciousness, nothing will change for the better... and the catastrophe towards which this world is headed – the ecological, social, demographic, or general breakdown of civilisation – will be unavoidable." Fortunately the inverse is also true: with a global revolution in the sphere of consciousness, the catastrophe towards which the world is headed is avoidable. As Mikhail Gorbachev points out in the Introduction, if we become conscious that a turning in human affairs is truly necessary and decide to do what we can, together we can accomplish all that is necessary.

Taking part in today's quiet but crucially important 'consciousness revolution' is your chance to change the world. Doing so calls for a different kind of growth: not growth in power and money, but in wholeness, awareness, and inner peace – that is, inner growth.

Paths to Inner Growth

Inner growth is a noble goal, but how are we to achieve it? There are people around us who have accomplished it. They have evolved a different way of thinking and acting and a more mature outlook. Many of them are people who have had unusual, life-transforming experiences. Astronauts had the privilege of seeing Earth from outer space and came back changed people. They have seen a precious world without boundaries that nourishes us, and gives a home to all human beings and to all nature. And they realised how petty and superficial it is to squabble over privileges and powers when we live on a planet unique in this corner of the universe.

Another life and mind transforming experience is the experience of coming back from the portals of death. People who have had a near-death experience return to everyday life with a deeply altered consciousness. Often they no longer fear dying. They achieve inner peace and have empathy for others and reverence for nature. They have a fresh appreciation of the wonder of existence.

Deep religious and spiritual experience is also conducive to a more developed consciousness. People who engage in intense meditation or prayer know that differences among people, whether due to sex, race, colour, language, political conviction or religious belief, do not mean that they are separate from us. They recognise that William James was right. We are like islands in the sea, separate on the surface but connected in the deep. There are levels of existence through which we do not simply communicate with each other – we actually become part of each other.

Becoming Whole

There are other, more accessible paths to inner growth as well. You can train your inner self to become more one with your outer self, achieving greater unity between body and mind. When you become whole, you can make the world around you whole.

Start with training yourself to become more at one with your body. Most of us have lost contact with our bodies. We are constantly occupied and preoccupied with tasks and aspirations, with hopes, fears and worries. We use our body as we use our car or computer: giving it commands to take us where we want to go and do what we want to have done. We live in our head, with little time and inclination to live in our whole body. We are losing the ground under our feet.

There are sophisticated methods that help us ground ourselves. They include traditional methods such as Tai Chi, Qi Gong, and Yoga, Ayurvedic and other holistic forms of exercise and massage, as well as new and old breathing techniques and techniques of deep relaxation. Even a simple exercise, practiced regularly, can help you achieve contact with your body.

Sit for a few minutes comfortably relaxed, with hands on knees and eyes closed. Concentrate on your body and feel it bit by bit, starting with the tips of your toes and ending with the top of your head. Become aware of your breathing – feel how every breath you take penetrates your lungs and makes energy course throughout your veins. Feel the rhythms of your body – the subtle movement of the muscles, the beating of the heart and the working of the organs. Soon you begin to feel your whole body, and begin to feel at home in it. You recover some of the sense of wholeness we have all lost in the stress and strain of everyday existence.

Grounding oneself in the body is the first step; it needs to be followed by another. The stresses and strains of existence also have an impact on our emotional life, and that too, needs attention. It is not that we would have lost contact with our emotions – we are only too aware of them most of the time. Only, they are often the wrong kind of emotions. Negative feelings such as anger, hate, fear, anxiety, suspicion, jealousy, contempt and indifference dominate the tenor of modern existence. They result from lifetime experiences that are mainly negative. With some exceptions, even childhood education is based on negative reinforcements such as punishment and the threat of failure. Positive emotions of love and caring are the preserve of the family and circle of friends, but these aspects of life are frequently sacrificed to pressure of work and the strain of securing our daily existence.

Positive emotions can also be generated by intimate experiences of nature: beholding the tranquillity of a sunny meadow or a calm lake, the beauty of a sunset, the majesty of a mountain, and the awesomeness of a stormy sea. For big-city people these experiences are few and far between. Even when they are accessible, in affluent circles they are often subordinated to the pursuit of social goals and aspirations, such as winning in a sport or impressing others with one's conversation and the latest fashion.

A vicious cycle holds most of us in its grip: negative experiences generate negative attitudes that create further negative experiences. This cycle must be broken. We need to take stock of our feelings, making a conscious effort to transform negative emotions. It is not easy to replace hate with love, suspicion with trust, contempt with respect, jealousy with appreciation and anxiety with self-assurance, yet it can be done. All the religions and spiritual traditions of the world offer ways to do it. There are also secular techniques. Group experiences can let us share our fears and hopes as can diverse psychotherapies, including re-living the experiences of our childhood, infancy, birth and even the womb.

If you make a sincere attempt at emotional purification, the vicious cycle of negative experiences generating more negative experiences will be replaced by a virtuous cycle of positive feelings toward others, generating understanding and empathy in collaborators, friends, family and fellow citizens.

Integrating mind and body and transforming our emotions are ends as well as means. They are valuable in themselves, and also serve as steps on the road to further growth. When we are grounded in our body and centred in our emotions we can open our body-mind to the world and receive the good things it can offer.

Growing with Art and Science

One of the good things our world can offer is culture. Culture is not the preserve of a privileged elite or the domain of people with formal education – its fruits and benefits are available to everyone. The domain of culture extends beyond museums, galleries, and concert halls; it is present throughout society. Culture shapes our cities through architecture and urban design, enters our feelings through music, entertains and triggers emotions via film, radio and television, and conveys new visions and deeper comprehension in literature and drama. It includes popular as well as high art, popular as well as serious literature, jazz, rock, and classical music, and poetry, dance, comedy and drama.

Whether of the high or the pop variety, art, music, theatre, and literature help us relate to others and to nature. They are an inexhaustible source of positive emotions, an inspiration for living, loving, and harmony with all of creation. At their best, they produce profound insight and intense emotion, reaching all the way to what psychologist Abraham Maslow called peak experiences. In our mobile and networked world these experiences are available to nearly everyone who values them and is serious about seeking them.

For advancing on the path to inner growth, science is another basic resource. This may come as a surprise: what does science have to do with our consciousness and personality? Modern science appears to be an abstract and abstruse collection of data, a repertory of cold and impersonal facts and measurements.

Moreover scientists use esoteric language and complex mathematics and their reports are neither accessible nor understandable beyond their disciplines. Science, most people believe, is useful as a source of technological innovation and is important in keeping our environment liveable and us alive, but beyond that it is of interest only to scientists.

This widespread view of science leaves out of account an aspect that is directly relevant to our personal development: the aspect of vision. Science is not only data and measurement, for scientists not only observe and measure: they also seek to discover how universe, life and mind are structured, and how they function. What they have been discovering in recent years inspires awe and wonder – it is very different from the scientific worldview we were taught at school. The ideas that dominate most people's mind have been overtaken by new discoveries. In the emerging view the universe is not a lifeless, soulless aggregate of inert chunks of matter: it is closer to a living organism. It is not matter that is the fundamental component of the universe: reality is made up of a variety of familiar as well as strange fields, forces and energies. Space and time are not a passive backdrop to the blind concourse of particles and atoms: they are the unified background of the evolution of galaxies. A cosmic energy and information field interlinks all parts of the universe and makes it an interacting, seamless whole.

Life is not a random accident in this self-evolving cosmos: it is part of its grand architecture of embracing harmony and supreme design. Our consciousness is an organic part of it as well. When you open your mind to the universe your consciousness will reflect its rhythms and harmonies, its forces and dynamics. You will resonate with the life-energies of the biosphere, and the evolving consciousness of humankind. [9]

When all is said and done, our shared destiny depends on the way you and people around you think and live. To think and live in a more responsible way you must be grounded in your body, centred in your emotions, and open to the many wonders of culture and nature around you. You then experience the wonder of life, instead of just the struggle for survival, wealth, and power.

If you want to be a part of the great stream that lifts humankind toward a positive future, look to yourself. You will grow up to be a more responsible individual, a better person with whom to share this planet and decide its future.

Notes

9. A detailed exposition of the worldview of cutting-edge science is given by the author in *The Creative Cosmos* (Floris Books, 1993), *The Interconnected Universe* (World Scientific, 1995), *The Whispering Pond* (Element Books, 1996), *The Connectivity Hypothesis* (State University of New York Press, 2003), and *The Holos Revolution* (in preparation).

Postscript

A Star to Follow

This action handbook has outlined the principal aspects of the necessary new thinking and the required responsible living. Now it adds another factor: a star on the horizon. This may seem like a 'far-out' factor, yet it is concrete and practical. The importance of having a star lies not in the possibility of reaching it, but in having it before our eyes to guide our steps.

Our star is the vision of the world in the year 2020. For our children, and for many among us, this vision could become living reality. Let us listen, then, as an inhabitant of the more evolved '2020 world' recounts how that world is organised, and how people think and live in it.

Message from a Peaceful Sustainable World

Place: Somewhere on the Six Continents   Date: 2020 AD
The Writer: A young woman born around the turn of the 21st century

The world I inhabit in the year 2020 is in many respects similar to the world I knew as a child, but for the most part, we are much happier. There are nearly 200 countries, some of them industrialised, others predominantly rural. Some of them make full use of the latest technologies, others prefer being guided by their traditions. There are two dozen giant cities but they are not growing any bigger. Most people live in medium-sized cities and towns, in rural communities or in eco-villages. People are just as diverse as at the turn of the century and since life is less stressful and more relaxed, cultural diversity comes even more to the fore than before. Wherever and however they live, people can pursue their ideals without having to compete on uniform global markets. North Americans and Latin Americans, Japanese, Chinese, Indians and all Asians, the same as all Europeans, Africans, Australians and Polynesians, can express their values and safeguard their traditions. They can choose their social structures, economic systems, personal aspirations and lifestyles free from the pressures of last century's one-sided globalisation.

This, however, is also a highly united world. Notwithstanding more autonomy and self-reliance, we have not fragmented the global community into isolated units pursuing separate goals without regard for the common good. Our diverse nations and cultures are united by common values and aspirations, centred on creating a world where all people can live safely and peacefully, without destroying the life-sustaining environment. Gone are the fears that dominated previous decades – fears of terrorism, armed conflict, economic breakdown, famine, ecological collapse and invasion by destitute migrants. Stability is the hallmark of our world. This is not the rigid stability imposed by a powerful authority, but the stability of a sustainably built network of self-reliant but co-operative communities, states, nations, and continental and global federations of nations.

Our System of Political Organisation

The 20th century's system of sovereign nation states has been transformed into a transnational system, organised as a series of administrative and decision-making forums, with each forum having its own sphere of competence. It is not a hierarchy, for the forums at the various levels have considerable autonomy and are not subordinated to the higher levels. In the areas of peace and security, the protection of the environment, information and communication, as well as finance, decision-making is global. But there is significant autonomy at local and regional levels. The 2020 world is a 'heterarchy': a multilevel structure of distributed decision-making. It is aimed at combining global co-ordination with local, regional and national autonomy.

Multiple links of communication and co-operation criss-cross our global system. Individuals jointly shape and develop their local communities. These communities participate in a wider network of co-operation that includes, but does not stop at, the level of nations. Nation-states in their turn are part of regional or continental social and economic federations.

For linking the world we have the United Peoples' Organisation, the body that succeeded the United Nations. The UPO observes, as do all other decision-making bodies of our world, the well-known but previously seldom respected 'principle of subsidiarity'. This means that decisions are made at the lowest level at which they are effective. The global level of the UPO, the world's highest level of decision making, is the lowest level at which peace and security can be safeguarded, the world environment cared for and the flow of money, technology and information across the continents can be regulated.

The UPO's political members are continental and subcontinental economic and social federations representing the shared interests of their member nations. They include the European Union, the North American Union, the Latin American Union, the North-African Middle-Eastern Union, the Sub-Saharan African Union, the Central Asian Union, the South and Southeast Asian Union and the Australian-Nippon-Pacific Union.

The United Peoples' Organisation also has members from civil society and business. Civil society members include representatives from various non-governmental organisations, active in social, economic and the environmental domains. Thanks to their membership the voice of the international NGO community is no longer foreign to policy-making in the world; it is an integral part of deliberations and decisions in all the relevant areas.

The corporate membership of the Organisation is made up of federations of businesses in the major branches of industry and commerce. Through specialised agencies in finance, industry, commerce, and labour, inherited from the United Nations and reformed in the light of the Organisation's enlarged mandate, the UPO connects its member business federations with the representatives of the communities in which they operate. It helps managers establish good community relations, create mutually agreed codes of conduct, and reach mutually beneficial agreements on trade, employment, finance, and the protection of the environment.

The World Environment Organisation, an affiliated member of the UPO, co-ordinates the environmental programmes of the continental and subcontinental federations. Global-level co-ordination is a precondition of successfully restoring the viability of the environment, re-establishing natural balances in the composition of air, water and soil, and preserving the integrity of biosphere's regenerative cycles.

The continental or subcontinental level is effective for co-ordinating the economic, social and political objectives and practices of nation-states. The economic and social federations provide a forum for the representatives of member nations to discuss their concerns, explore areas of mutual interest, and seek co-operative agreements and projects.

The tasks and responsibilities of nation-states have not changed significantly. National governments remain the principal arbiters of their country's economic and social objectives. Nation-states maintain a national treasury, a national judicial system, police force and health system. But these institutions do not operate under the premise of absolute sovereignty. Domestically, they are integrated with the administrations of cities and rural areas and internationally, with the structures and policies of other states in the federation to which the nation belongs.

The local level of co-ordination and decision-making serves cities, towns and villages. At this level direct democracy is the rule. The representatives of the people respond directly to the people. The customary mechanism is the town hall meeting, held face to face whenever and wherever possible, and electronically when distance or cost prevents a significant number of people from participating.

Our System of Economic Organisation

The economic systems of nation-states are different in detail, but they rest on the same fundamental principles. One of these principles is the belief that the ultimate source of all our wealth on Earth is the Earth itself. The biological and mineral resources of the planet are the principal assets of human economies.

Another shared principle is that basic needs must be satisfied for all people regardless of age and sex, and whether or not they are physically or mentally able to engage in remunerated work.

National economies seek their own balance between market forces, the valuation of natural assets and social welfare. Some countries provide a guaranteed income for their people in order to assure that they can meet their basic needs. Previously unpaid work, such as maintaining a household, caring for others and for the environment and growing one's own food is recognised to be socially and economically useful. In this way people in the majority of today's nation-states do not depend on competing in the market for staple food, shelter and basic education. They can choose their preferred work or profession free of existential concerns.

Given that we hold our greatest capital asset to be the natural world, the sustainability of this world is not utopian. With changed values and lifestyles came changed patterns of consumption, resulting in lower energy and material requirements and more modest and efficient use of energy and raw materials. Thanks to efficient use of resources, less waste and simpler lifestyles, the size of the ecological footprint of individuals and the collective footprint of cities and economies is dropping in all parts of the world. The average footprint is approaching long-term sustainability: it is not much more than two hectares per person.

Business and politics are no longer at odds. Without dictates from above, the private sector is becoming a voluntary part of civil society. In line with our shared valuation of nature as the source of all our assets, the paramount philosophy of business is not the increase of shareholder value through the company-centred exploitation of the available resources, but the shared ethic of trusteeship of wealth-producing assets. Business managers, like many business leaders in the 19th and early 20th century, are concerned to assure success for their companies but they also seek a role among the builders of society. They endeavour to overcome the tension between efficiency, profitability and dynamism on the one hand, and solidarity, equity and sustainability on the other. They select products and services to bring to the market in consultation with their clients and customers, as well as with their employees and partners. Even if production and marketing decisions remain informed by considerations of success in the marketplace, they are also informed by regard for environmental impact, employee satisfaction and the actual usefulness of the products and services the company places on the market. In consequence much of the wastefulness of last century's throwaway culture is eliminated; built-in obsolescence has become obsolete in itself.

The world's monetary system has undergone much-needed reform at all levels – global, regional and local. The biggest change is that today no money is issued on the basis of debt. Instead, it is spent or given into circulation. This makes economic life much more stable because the amount of money passing from hand to hand no longer declines if businesses or consumers decide not to borrow as much this year as they did twelve months ago.

Another change is that we no longer use national currencies as if they were global ones. The UPO issued the world currency, the Gaia, by giving it to every continent on the basis of its population rather than its economic strength. The amount of Gaias in circulation is regulated so that the total amount of economic activity going on around the globe is compatible with the environment's ability to cope. If we are putting too big a volume of greenhouse gases into the atmosphere risking climate change, we bring the number of Gaias down so that global trade operates at a lower level. This does not mean that the economic and social federations are limited in the amount of their economic activity. The massive switch to renewable energy has led to a long running economic boom and the federations find ways of further boosting their economies whilst using less fossil fuel.

The federations have their own currencies which they spend into circulation and take back through tax. Their currencies are used for trade between a federation's member states; the Gaia is reserved for inter-federation transfers. City regions also have their own currencies as do many towns and villages. The latter are usually run by the community rather than by the local government. The big advantage of the system is its flexibility. When moving around it is easy to swap one currency for another at the agreed exchange rate while local people always have enough cash to trade with each other, even if they cannot buy luxuries from elsewhere.

These two changes – the restriction on fossil fuel use and the development of a diversity of currencies – has led to a re-localisation of economic life. Life may be hard in some places but, almost everywhere, people have escaped poverty, dependency and marginalisation and are developing vibrant economies and cultures of their own.

Our Use of Technology

Technology is no longer valued for itself. The peoples of the year 2020 seek to make technology their servant rather than master. Most of the presently used technologies are more advanced than the early 21st century technologies, but not all technologies that are available are actually put to use. Social utility and environmental friendliness are major factors in choosing which we decide to develop.

The most important technological advance is in the way we source our energy. We have eliminated risky nuclear reactors and greatly reduced our use of fossil fuels. Nearly half of our energies come from the sun, as a direct source through photovoltaic and solar thermal technologies and indirectly, in the form of hydropower, wind, wave and tidal energy, geothermal and biomass. Our entry into the 'solar age' not only brings a practically infinite source of energy without polluting air, land and water, but also helps re-balance the world's economies in favour of global economic prosperity as solar and solar-related energy sources exist almost everywhere on the six continents.

There are great advances in life sustaining technologies. In the sphere of classical medicine, invasive technologies are limited to cases of birth defects, accidents and serious malady. A softer and more holistic approach predominates in most other cases. The accent is on the maintenance of health through the prevention of disease, and this requires that we consider the human being as an integrated whole of body and soul, and an integral part of his and her society, culture and environment. The techniques that foster our inner development are an offshoot of our holistic approach to health. These 'soft technologies', combining ancient methods with new biomedical and psychophysical methods, are recognised adjuncts to human growth and development. They are widespread and widely accepted.

In the areas of industrial production, current technologies concentrate on producing what is needed and beneficial without creating adverse side effects. There have been great improvements in recycling industrial and household wastes, and in eliminating by-products that pollute air, land and water.

In agriculture the emphasis is on maintaining biological diversity and producing a safe and sustainable supply of basic foods. We realise that the human body is part of terrestrial nature and natural foods are the best suited to maintaining its health and vigour. In addition to food production, agriculture is a source of natural energies and raw materials. Plants such as hemp grow prolifically almost everywhere and they offer a renewable raw material for producing paper, textiles and oil as well as some new varieties of plastics.

Much effort is devoted to ensuring a sustainable supply of clean water. In arid parts of the world, traditional sources are supplemented by desalinating seawater but a worldwide programme to restore the earth and replant our forests has helped to reduce droughts and rebalance the climate.

Our transport technologies aim at reconciling the requirement for mobility with the requirement for personal safety and public health. This is much less of a problem than it was at the turn of the century, for the emphasis on local self-reliance and autonomy reduced the need for people and goods to move long distances. The valuation of natural assets has been another factor: it made us aware that energy, even if renewable, is a precious resource to be used with care, and that transport systems, even when ecological, have an unavoidable negative impact on nature. This impact is limited, but not totally eliminated, by the use of clean renewable energies, such as plant-based fuels, liquid hydrogen, electricity, fuel cells, compressed air and various hybrid motive technologies adapted to local conditions and requirements.

The communication technologies in use today are not substantially different from those of the early years of the century.

Hardware is smaller, cheaper and more powerful, and software is both simpler and more effective, adapted to use by people in all walks of life. Computers are at work in many facets of daily life and work. They eliminate some chores and make others easier, but they do not revolutionalise our existence in the way technological forecasters and science fiction writers envisaged. We still live on Earth in human communities within the embrace of nature. We make use of technology to live better and more sustainably.

A major change in the use of technology occurred in the aftermath of the deepening conflicts and escalating wars of the first decades of the century. The leaders and peoples of the world realised that there are no reliable measures to prevent technologies intended for defence, being used for aggression with disastrous consequences. Since it was not feasible to eliminate powerful weapons systems from the arsenal of any nation or region as long as others possessed them, the members of the United Peoples Organisation decreed worldwide disarmament, with implementation vested in the continental and sub-continental federations. In consequence, in the armaments field, research and development focuses not on producing more potent devices for killing and destruction, but on more effective and reliable ways to verify that they are not being produced by any nation or group in the world.

There has been a corresponding de-escalation in the civic use of weapons. Criminality and violence are at a low level, thanks to improved social conditions and more balanced development in the economic sphere. With a lower level of frustration there is less resentment and hate, and the near-inaccessibility of lethal weapons reduces the incidence of gang-wars, massive killings and organised crime. There is no longer need for large, highly equipped police forces and high-security prisons. With the exception of special forces, law-enforcement officers are equipped much as 20th century English policemen – with rubber sticks and handcuffs, occasionally supplemented by temporarily disabling sprays and non-lethal lasers.

Our Ways of Living

Although more and more people prefer a co-operative approach to work and business, people can opt to become entrepreneurs running their own businesses. If they are successful, they become richer than most others. But whether people are rich or poor, they live more simply than the rich lived at the beginning of the 21st century. They adopt simpler lifestyles because of a deeper sense of responsibility for themselves, their neighbours and their environment, and not just because legislation and taxes offer economic incentives for them.

People do not believe that living well calls for ostentation. Living well means living comfortably, in some cases even luxuriously, but luxury does not lie in hoarding material goods but in achieving a high quality of lived experience. The dominant aspiration is personal rather than economic growth. It is the growth of intellectual and emotional life, achieved not in the isolation of a private dwelling, whether mansion or hut, but in the embrace of family, community and country, and the global community of all peoples and countries.

As we join together to improve the quality of our living and working environment, community life enjoys a renaissance. There is a renaissance of spirituality as well. More and more women and men rediscover a higher and deeper dimension of their life. With 'localisation' balancing globalisation, and daily existence becoming more assured, there is less pressure on people, leaving more time for family, community and nature, and for spiritual concerns.

People live longer and healthier lives, but the population of the world is not growing beyond the current level of eight billion. Longer lifespans are offset by smaller families as people realise that it is irresponsible to produce children beyond levels of replacement. This has obvious benefits. With modest sized families we are able to take better care of our children, ensuring that they grow into healthy individuals, with sufficient education to think well and live sustainably within the embrace of society and nature.

A Personal Comment

The changes I have just recounted in our political, economic and social systems, our use of technology and our lifestyles, are not temporary trends or fads and they do not obey the dictates of a higher authority. They result from the new mindset that emerged in my generation. This consciousness is in some ways very different from that which dominated my childhood in the early years of this century.

There are many things that differentiate the people of the Earth as we head into the third decade of the 21st century: religious beliefs, cultural heritage, economic and technological de-velopment, climate and environment. But even if we are culturally, geographically and economically diverse, our more evolved consciousness makes it possible for us to agree on some of the things that are truly fundamental.

We know, and feel with every cell of our body, that all eight billion of us are inhabitants of this planet, and all have a right to its resources and its life-supporting environment.

We are convinced that it is immoral for any of us to live in a way that detracts from the chances of the rest of us to achieve a life of basic well-being and human dignity.

We believe that the universal rights adopted by our forebears in the 20th century – the right to freedom of expression, freedom to elect our leaders, and freedom from torture and other arbitrary constraints on personal liberty, as well as the right to food, shelter, education, and employment – apply to everyone in the global community and deserve to be respected above and beyond considerations of personal, ethnic and national self-interest.

We realise that it is more effective to exercise responsible trusteeship over the human and natural sources of wealth on this planet than to exploit them for narrow and short-term benefit.

We have come to the insight that nature is not a mechanism to be engineered and exploited, but a living system that brought us into being, that nourishes us and, given our awesome powers of exploitation and destruction, is now entrusted to our care.

We learned that the way to solve our problems and conflicts is not by attacking each other, but by understanding one another and cooperating in ways that serve our joint interests.

Finally, we have understood that what we think and how we live shapes our present and decides our future. The alternative to a world of misery, conflict and violence is a sustainable and equitable world that inspires peace in people's hearts – the precondition of lasting peace on Earth.

Appendices

The Manifesto on Planetary Consciousness

A new way of thinking has become the necessary condition for responsible living and acting. Evolving it means fostering creativity in all people, in all parts of the world. Creativity is not a genetic but a cultural endowment of human beings. Culture and society change fast but genes change slowly. No more than one half of one percent of the human genetic endowment is likely to alter in a century and hence, most of our genes date from the Stone Age or before. They could help us to live in the jungles of nature but not in the jungles of civilisation. Today's economic, social and technological environment is our own creation, and only the creativity of our minds – our culture, spirit, and consciousness – will enable us to cope with it. Genuine creativity does not remain paralysed when faced with unusual and unexpected problems but confronts them openly, without prejudice. Cultivating it is a precondition of finding our way toward a globally interconnected society in which individuals, enterprises, states, and the whole family of peoples and nations could live together peacefully, cooperatively, and with mutual benefit.

A Call for Responsibility

In the course of the 20th century, people in many parts of the world have become conscious of their rights as well as of many persistent violations of them. This development is important, but in itself it is not enough. We must now become conscious of the factor without which neither rights nor other values can be effectively safeguarded: our individual and collective responsibilities. We are not likely to grow into a peaceful and co-operative human family unless we become responsible social, economic, political, and cultural actors.

We human beings need more than food, water, and shelter. We need more even than remunerated work, self-esteem and social acceptance. We also need something to live for: an ideal to achieve, a responsibility to accept. Because we are aware of the consequences of our actions, we can and must accept responsibility for them. Such responsibility goes deeper than many of us may think. In today's world all people, no matter where they live and what they do, have become responsible for their actions as: private individuals, citizens, collaborators in business and the economy, members of the human community and persons endowed with mind and consciousness.

As individuals, we are responsible for seeking our interests in harmony with the interests and well being of others. We are responsible for condemning and averting any form of killing and brutality; responsible for not bringing more children into the world than we truly need and can support; and responsible for respecting the right to life, development, and equal status and dignity of all the children, women, and men who inhabit the Earth.

As citizens, we are responsible for demanding that our leaders beat swords into ploughshares and relate to other nations peacefully and in a spirit of co-operation; that they recognise the legitimate aspirations of all communities in the human family; and that they do not abuse sovereign powers to manipulate people and the environment for shortsighted and selfish ends.

As collaborators in business and the economy, we are responsible for ensuring that commercial objectives do not centre uniquely on profit and growth but include a concern that products and services respond to human needs and demands without harming people and impairing nature; that they do not serve destructive ends and unscrupulous designs; and that they respect the rights of all entrepreneurs and enterprises who compete fairly in the global marketplace.

As members of the human community, it is our responsibility to adopt a culture of non-violence, solidarity, and economic, political, and social equality, promoting mutual understanding and respect among people and nations whether they are like us or different, demanding that all people everywhere should be empowered to respond to the challenges that face them with the material as well as spiritual resources that are required for this unprecedented task.

And as persons endowed with mind and consciousness, our responsibility is to encourage comprehension and appreciation for the excellence of the human spirit in all its manifestations, and for inspiring awe and wonder for a cosmos that brought forth life and consciousness and holds out the possibility of its continued evolution toward ever higher levels of insight, understanding, love, and compassion.

A Call for Planetary Consciousness

In most parts of the world, the real potential of human beings is sadly underdeveloped. The way children are raised depresses their faculties for learning and creativity; the way young people experience the struggle for material survival results in frustration and resentment. In adults this leads to a variety of compensatory, addictive, and compulsive behaviours. The result is the persistence of social and political oppression, economic warfare, cultural intolerance, crime, and disregard for the environment.

Eliminating social and economic ills and frustrations calls for considerable socio-economic development, and that is not possible without better education, information, and communication. These, however, are blocked by the absence of socio-economic development, so that a vicious cycle is produced: under-development creates frustration, and frustration, giving rise to defective behaviours, blocks development. This cycle must be broken at its point of greatest flexibility, that is the development of the spirit and consciousness of human beings. Achieving this objective does not pre-empt the need for socio-economic development with all its financial and technical resources, but calls for a parallel mission in the spiritual field. Unless people's spirit and consciousness evolve to the planetary dimension, the processes that stress the globalised society-nature system will intensify and create a shock wave that could jeopardise the entire transition towards a peaceful and co-operative global society. This would be a setback for humanity and a danger for everyone. Evolving human spirit and consciousness is the first vital cause shared by the whole of the human family.

Planetary consciousness is knowing, as well as feeling, the vital interdependence and essential oneness of humankind. It is the conscious adoption of the ethic and the ethos that this entails. Its evolution is the basic imperative of human survival on this planet.

Manifesto drafted by Ervin Laszlo in consultation
with the Dalai Lama and adopted by the Club of Budapest
on October 26, 1996.

The Wise Response to Violence

The 11th September suicide attack on New York's World Trade Centre and Washington's Pentagon was an offence against all of human life and every civilisation. We condemn this act of terrorism and call to ethical and peace-loving people the world over to join together to put an end to terrorism and violence in all its forms. There is no solution to the world's problems by killing innocent people and destroying their workplaces and habitations.

If we are to succeed in eradicating violence and terrorism from the world, we must act wisely. Violence and terrorism will not be vanquished by retaliation on the principle of eye for an eye and tooth for a tooth. The ultimate roots of violence lie deeper than the fanatic commitment of terrorists and the religious claims of fundamentalists. Killing one group of terrorists will not solve the problem: as long as the roots are there, others will grow in their place.

The terror that surfaces in today's world is a symptom of longstanding and deep-seated frustrations, resentment, and perceived injustice, and eliminating the symptom does not cure the malady. The Club of Budapest is committed to search for the causes of violence in the world. Until and unless the causes are eliminated there will not be peace in the world, only an uncertain interlude between acts of violence and larger-scale hostilities. When people are frustrated, harbour hate and the desire for revenge, they cannot relate to each other in a spirit of peace and cooperation. Whether the cause is the wounded ego of a person or the wounded self-respect of a people, and whether it is the wish for personal revenge or a holy war for the defence of a faith, the result is violence, death, and catastrophe. Attaining peace in people's heart is a precondition of attaining peace in the world.

The Club of Budapest maintains that the wise response to violence and terrorism is to help people to be at peace with themselves and their fellow humans near and far. Promoting solidarity and cooperation in the shared cause of fairness and justice is the only feasible path to lasting peace on Earth.

Declaration adopted by the Club of Budapest on September 23, 2001.

Declaration for All Life on Earth

The Earth is an evolving living entity. Every form of life on earth is an important part of this living entity. Accordingly, we, as individual human beings, must cultivate the awareness that we are all members of a global community of life and that we share a common mission and responsibility for the future of our planet.

Every one of us has a role to play in the evolution of our planet, and to achieve world peace each of us must live up to our responsibilities and obligations. Up to the present time, few people on earth have been fully satisfied with life. We have faced conflicts all over the world in competition for limited resources and land. This has had a devastating effect on the global environment.

As we enter the new millennium, more than anything else, the realisation of world peace depends on an awakening of consciousness on the part of each individual member of the human race. Today, it is imperative that every human being bears the responsibility of building peace and harmony in his or her heart. We all have this common mission that we must fulfil. World peace will be achieved when every member of humanity becomes aware of this common mission – when we all join together for our common purpose.

Until now, in terms of power, wealth, fame, knowledge, technology and education, humanity has been divided between individuals, nations and organisations that have possession and those that do not. There have also been distinctions between the givers and the receivers, the helpers and the helped.

We hereby declare our commitment to transcend all these dualities and distinctions with a totally new concept, which will serve as our foundation as we set out to build a peaceful world.

General Principles

In the new era, humanity shall advance toward a world of harmony, that is, a world in which every individual and every nation can freely express their individual qualities, while living in harmony with one another and with all life on earth. To realise this vision, we set forth the following guiding principles:

1 Reverence for life
We shall create a world based on love and harmony in which all forms of life are respected.

2 Respect for all differences
We shall create a world in which all different races, ethnic groups, religions, cultures, traditions and customs are respected. The world must be a place free from discrimination or confrontation, socially, physically and spiritually – a place where diversity is appreciated and enjoyed.

3 Gratitude for and coexistence with all of nature
We shall create a world in which each person is aware that we are enabled to live through the blessings of nature, and lives in harmony with nature, showing gratitude for all animal, plant and other forms of life.

4 Harmony between the spiritual and material
We shall create a world based on the harmonious balance of material and spiritual civilisation. We must break away from our overemphasis on the material to allow a healthy spirituality to

blossom among humanity. We must build a world where not only material abundance but also spiritual riches are valued.

Practice

We shall put these principles into practice guided by the following:

As Individuals:

We must move beyond an era in which authority and responsibility rest in nation states, ethnic groups and religions to one in which the individual is paramount. We envision an 'Age of the Individual' – not in the sense of egoism, but an age in which every individual is ready to accept responsibility and to carry out his or her mission as an independent member of the human race.

Each of us shall carry out our greatest mission to bring love, harmony and gratitude into our own heart, and in so doing, bring harmony to the world at large.

In our Specialised Fields:

We shall build a system of cooperation in which wisdom is gathered together to derive the most from technical knowledge, skills and ability in various fields, such as education, science, culture and the arts, as well as religion, philosophy, politics and economics.

As the Young Generation:

In the 20th century, parents, teachers and society were the educators of children, and the children were always in the position of being taught. In the 21st century, adults shall learn from the wonderful qualities of children, such as their purity, innocence, radiance, wisdom and intuition, to inspire and uplift one another. The young generation shall play a leading role in the creation of peace for a bright future. May Peace Prevail on Earth.

Declaration adopted by the Goi Peace Foundation
of Tokyo, Japan

The Earth Charter

We stand at a critical moment in Earth's history, a time when humanity must choose its future. As the world becomes increasingly interdependent and fragile, the future at once holds great peril and great promise. To move forward we must recognise that in the midst of a magnificent diversity of cultures and life forms we are one human family and one Earth community with a common destiny. We must join together to bring forth a sustainable global society founded on respect for nature, universal human rights, economic justice, and a culture of peace. Towards this end, it is imperative that we, the peoples of Earth, declare our responsibility to one another, to the greater community of life, and to future generations.

Earth, Our Home

Humanity is part of a vast evolving universe. Earth, our home, is alive with a unique community of life. The forces of nature make existence a demanding and uncertain adventure, but Earth has provided the conditions essential to life's evolution. The resilience of the community of life and the well-being of humanity depend upon preserving a healthy biosphere with all its ecological systems, a rich variety of plants and animals, fertile soils, pure waters, and clean air. The global environment with its finite resources is a common concern of all peoples. The protection of Earth's vitality, diversity, and beauty is a sacred trust.

The Global Situation

The dominant patterns of production and consumption are causing environmental devastation, the depletion of resources, and a massive extinction of species. Communities are being undermined.

The benefits of development are not shared equitably and the gap between rich and poor is widening. Injustice, poverty, ignorance, and violent conflict are widespread and the cause of great suffering. An unprecedented rise in human population has over-burdened ecological and social systems. The foundations of global security are threatened. These trends are perilous – but not inevitable.

The Challenges Ahead

The choice is ours: form a global partnership to care for Earth and one another or risk the destruction of ourselves and the diversity of life. Fundamental changes are needed in our values, institutions, and ways of living. We must realise that when basic needs have been met, human development is primarily about being more, not having more. We have the knowledge and technology to provide for all and to reduce our impacts on the environment. The emergence of a global civil society is creating new opportunities to build a democratic and humane world. Our environmental, economic, political, social, and spiritual challenges are interconnected, and together we can forge inclusive solutions.

Universal Responsibility

To realise these aspirations, we must decide to live with a sense of universal responsibility, identifying ourselves with the whole Earth community as well as our local communities. We are at once citizens of different nations and of one world in which the local and global are linked. Everyone shares responsibility for the present and future well-being of the human family and the larger living world. The spirit of human solidarity and kinship with all life is strengthened when we live with reverence for the mystery of being, gratitude for the gift of life, and humility regarding the human place in nature.

Excerpted from the Earth Charter [www.earthcharter.org]

Toward A Global Ethic

The Principles of a Global Ethic

Our world is experiencing a fundamental crisis: A crisis in global economy, global ecology, and global politics. The lack of a grand vision, the tangle of unresolved problems, political paralysis, mediocre political leadership with little insight or foresight, and in general too little sense for the commonweal are seen everywhere: too many old answers to new challenges.

Hundreds of millions of human beings on our planet increasingly suffer from unemployment, poverty, hunger, and the destruction of their families. Hope for a lasting peace among nations slips away from us. There are tensions between the sexes and generations. Children die, kill, and are killed. More and more countries are shaken by corruption in politics and business. It is increasingly difficult to live together peacefully in our cities because of social, racial, and ethnic conflicts, the abuse of drugs, organised crime, and even anarchy. Even neighbours often live in fear of one another. Our planet continues to be ruthlessly plundered. A collapse of the ecosystem threatens us.

Time and again we see leaders and members of religions incite aggression, fanaticism, hate, and xenophobia – even inspire and legitimise violent and bloody conflicts. Religion often is misused for purely power-political goals, including war. We are filled with disgust.

We condemn these blights and declare that they need not be. An ethic already exists within the religious teachings of the world, which can counter the global distress. Of course this ethic provides no direct solution for all the immense problems of the world, but it does supply the moral foundation for a better individual and global order: A vision which can lead women and men away from despair, and society away from chaos.

We are persons who have committed ourselves to the precepts and practices of the world's religions.We confirm that there is already a consensus among the religions which can be the basis for a global ethic – a minimal fundamental consensus concerning binding values, irrevocable standards, and fundamental moral attitudes.

No New Global Order Without a New Global Ethic!

We women and men of various religions and regions of Earth therefore address all people, religious and non-religious. We wish to express the following convictions, which we hold in common:

- We all have a responsibility for a better global order.
- Our involvement for the sake of human rights, freedom, justice, peace, and the preservation of Earth is absolutely necessary.
- Our different religious and cultural traditions must not prevent our common involvement in opposing all forms of inhumanity and working for greater humaneness.
- The principles expressed in this Global Ethic can be affirmed by all persons with ethical convictions, whether religiously grounded or not.
- As religious and spiritual persons we base our lives on an Ultimate Reality, and draw spiritual power and hope therefrom, in trust, in prayer or meditation, in word or silence. We have a special responsibility for the welfare of all humanity and care for the planet Earth. We do not consider ourselves better than other women and men, but we trust that the ancient wisdom of our religions can point the way for the future.

After two world wars and the end of the cold war, the collapse of fascism and nazism, the shaking to the foundations of communism and colonialism, humanity has entered a new phase of its history. Today we possess sufficient economic, cultural, and spiritual resources to introduce a better global order. But old and new ethnic, national, social, economic, and religious tensions threaten the peaceful building of a better world. We have experienced greater technological progress than ever before, yet we see that world-wide poverty, hunger, death of children, unemployment, misery, and the destruction of nature have not diminished but rather have increased. Many peoples are threatened with economic ruin, social disarray, political marginalisation, ecological catastrophe, and national collapse.

In such a dramatic global situation humanity needs a vision of peoples living peacefully together, of ethnic and ethical groupings and of religions sharing responsibility for the care of Earth. A vision rests on hopes, goals, ideals, standards. But all over the world these have slipped from our hands. Yet we are convinced that, despite their frequent abuses and failures, it is the communities of faith who bear a responsibility to demonstrate that such hopes, ideals, and standards can be guarded, grounded, and lived. This is especially true in the modern state. Guarantees of freedom of conscience and religion are necessary but they do not substitute for binding values, convictions, and norms, which are valid for all humans regardless of their social origin, sex, skin colour, language, or religion.

We are convinced of the fundamental unity of the human family on Earth. We recall the 1948 Universal Declaration of Human Rights of the United Nations. What it formally proclaimed on the level of rights we wish to confirm and deepen here from the perspective of an ethic: The full realisation of the intrinsic dignity of the human person, the inalienable freedom and equality in principle of all humans, and the necessary solidarity and interdependence of all humans with each other.

On the basis of personal experiences and the burdensome history of our planet we have learned

- that a better global order cannot be created or enforced by laws, prescriptions, and conventions alone;
- that the realisation of peace, justice, and the protection of Earth depends on the insight and readiness of men and women to act justly;
- that action in favour of rights and freedoms presumes a consciousness of responsibility and duty, and that therefore both the minds and hearts of women and men must be addressed;
- that rights without morality cannot long endure, and that there will be no better global order without a global ethic.

By a global ethic we do not mean a global ideology or a single unified religion beyond all existing religions, and certainly not the domination of one religion over all others. By a global ethic we mean a fundamental consensus on binding values, irrevocable standards, and personal attitudes. Without such a fundamental consensus on an ethic, sooner or later every community will be threatened by chaos or dictatorship, and individuals will despair.

A Transformation of Consciousness

Historical experience demonstrates the following: Earth cannot be changed for the better unless we achieve a transformation in the consciousness of individuals and in public life. The possibilities for transformation have already been glimpsed in areas such as war and peace, economy, and ecology, where in recent decades fundamental changes have taken place. This transformation must also be achieved in the area of ethics and values! Every individual has intrinsic dignity and inalienable rights, and each also has an inescapable responsibility for what she or he does and does not do. All our decisions and deeds, even our omissions and failures, have consequences.

Keeping this sense of responsibility alive, deepening it and passing it on to future generations, is the special task of religions. We are realistic about what we have achieved in this consensus, and so we urge that the following be observed:

1 A universal consensus on many disputed ethical questions (from bio and sexual ethics through mass media and scientific ethics to economic and political ethics) will be difficult to attain. Nevertheless, even for many controversial questions, suitable solutions should be attainable in the spirit of the fundamental principles we have jointly developed here.

2 In many areas of life a new consciousness of ethical responsibility has already arisen. Therefore we would be pleased if as many professions as possible, such as those of physicians, scientists, business people, journalists, and politicians, would develop up-to-date codes of ethics which would provide specific guidelines for the vexing questions of these particular professions.

3 Above all, we urge the various communities of faith to formulate their very specific ethics: What does each faith tradition have to say for example, about the meaning of life and death, the enduring of suffering and the forgiveness of guilt, about selfless sacrifice and the necessity of renunciation, about

compassion and joy? These will deepen, and make more specific, the already discernible global ethic.

In conclusion, we appeal to all the inhabitants of this planet. Earth cannot be changed for the better unless the consciousness of individuals is changed. We pledge to work for such transformation in individual and collective consciousness, for the awakening of our spiritual powers through reflection, meditation, prayer, or positive thinking, for a conversion of the heart. Together we can move mountains! Without a willingness to take risks and a readiness to sacrifice there can be no fundamental change in our situation! Therefore we commit ourselves to a common global ethic, to better mutual understanding, as well as to socially beneficial, peace-fostering, and Earth-friendly ways of life.

We invite all men and women, whether religious or not, to do the same!

Declaration excerpted from the Declaration of the Parliament of World Religions, Chicago, 1993

The Activities and Mission of the Club of Budapest

Reported by Peter Spiegel, General Secretary

The Club of Budapest, founded in 1993 by Ervin Laszlo, is an informal association of ethical opinion leaders active globally, as well as locally, in various fields of art, science, religion, and culture, dedicated to our common future. Its members include the Dalai Lama, Václav Havel, Mikhail Gorbachev, Desmond Tutu, Elie Wiesel, Peter Ustinov, Peter Gabriel, and young and creative people in many parts of the world. They place their name and energy into the service of what they consider the crucial mission of our time: catalysing the emergence of adapted vision and values in society by evolving our individual and collective consciousness.

The Club is part of a far-reaching network of organisations that form what is now called 'global civil society.' Its own mission and activities are briefly described below.

From Think-Tank to Catalyst for Change
The 'cultural creatives' – people with a developed 'planetary consciousness' – the avant-garde of global civil society, first emerged into prominence in 1972, when the Club of Rome

published *The Limits to Growth*. This report gave a major boost to the growing worldwide environmental movement and a critical social consciousness. But human and organisational limits soon became apparent. Ervin Laszlo pointed to these limits in his 1978 book *The Inner Limits of Mankind*.

The members of the Club of Rome were recruited mainly from the scientific, political and economic spheres of society. Art, culture and religion, with their origins in the more creative and intuitive right side of the brain, were hardly represented. To fill this need, in 1993 Ervin Laszlo, one of the first members of the Club of Rome, founded the Club of Budapest. This sister-club, made up of personalities such as the Dalai Lama, Peter Ustinov, and Yehudi Menuhin, had a new holistic planetary consciousness as its aim. Later the Club also embraced personalities, such as Mikhail Gorbachev, Richard von Weizsäcker, Mary Robinson and Muhammad Yunus, who exemplify a more rationally-based but equally responsible and ethical way of thinking and acting.

The non-governmental organisations of global civil society movement in the seventies and eighties had a strong orientation towards protest. This gave them an important role as the 'conscience of mankind' but at the cost of neglecting the positive human orientation required for creative solutions to the problems facing the global family. Only in the recent past has it been realised that we cannot rely only upon politicians and economists to lead us toward a positive future – all aspects of human existence need careful examination. This realisation defines the need for, and the mission of, the Club of Budapest.

In order to respond to this mission, the Club engages in a multifaceted set of activities in co-operation with a number of likeminded organisations.

Publications and the Planetary Vision Festival

You Can Change the World is the motto that expresses the basic principle on which the Club bases its projects. The *Handbook for the 21st Century,* now in the hands of the reader, provides practical and ethical guidance for everyone who wishes to join the global civil-society movement for better ethics and a planetary consciousness. It will be followed by a series of books, as well as innovative programmes on the internet, video, radio and television.

The Planetary Vision Festival of the Club of Budapest celebrated the dawning of the first Spring day of the Third Millennium by proclaiming the 22nd of March 2001 'World Day of Planetary Consciousness.' In 28 locations worldwide, ranging from New Zealand to Japan, China, and India, as well as Europe, USA, Canada, Mexico, Brazil and Samoa, multi-cultural celebrations took place that followed the rise of the Sun around the globe. *Tomorrow Today,* a TV-documentary moderated by Peter Ustinov, documents the vision, culture, and significance of this initiative. The Dalai Lama, Peter Gabriel, Jane Goodall, Peter Russell and Sir Arthur Clark are among the Club of Budapest members commenting on the events.

The World Day of Planetary Consciousness, together with the World Day of Planetary Ethics, are celebrated each year, hosted by the Club of Budapest in partnership with likeminded organisations in many parts of the world.

The Survey of 'Cultural Creatives'

Decisive for the success of any movement towards a more peaceful and sustainable world is to identify the people who are able and willing to champion the new values and adopt the corresponding behaviour. Who are the agents of local and global change? On the basis of studies by Ervin Laszlo and other members of the Club, two sets of projects seek to answer this question. The first looks at the values and behaviour already evolving in civil society. In 1999, a member of the Club of Budapest, Paul Ray together with Sherry Ruth Anderson, carried out a much-discussed survey to identify the emerging culture known as the 'cultural creatives' in the United States. They showed that one quarter of the US adult population is leaving behind both the traditionalist and modernist mainstream cultures and espousing holistic and responsible values and lifestyles. The cultural creatives are not limited to the 'New Age' subculture – its members include all religious orientations and come from all walks of life.

If the processes of change are to be given the impetus needed to make an impact on society, the movement of the cultural creatives must be studied and identified in many parts of the world. The Club of Budapest is organising a survey on current changes in values, opinions and lifeways in Europe (in Germany, France, Italy, Poland, and Hungary) to be followed by similar surveys in the East (initially in Japan).

A second project of the Club focuses on a special subgroup within the culture of the creatives, the 'social entrepreneurs'. This group is made up partly of entrepreneurs who have turned towards social and ecological problems using their economic and organisational competence, and partly of civil society activists who are adopting entrepreneurial thinking and developing entrepreneurial skills. Both have come up with creative and successful innovations in recent years. The power of innovation represented by the new generation of social entrepreneurs, the Club believes, is significant and merits being recognised by all strata of society.

The 'Change the World' Planetary Consciousness Prize and Best Practice Award

One of the strongest motivations for a change of consciousness is to highlight individuals who have accomplished this change and have earned the respect of the world around them. Each year the Club of Budapest nominates for the Planetary Consciousness Prize outstanding personalities whose life and work has been hallmarked by this more evolved consciousness. Since 1996 annual Planetary Consciousness Prizes in the World Leadership category have been given to Vaclav Havel, Mikhail Gorbachev, Desmond Tutu, Kofi Annan, and Shimon Peres; the Planetary Consciousness Business Leadership Prize has been presented to Grameen bank founder and micro-credit innovator Mohammed Yunus; and the Planetary Consciousness Literature Prize has been awarded to Brazilian author Paolo Coelho.

Through a specially constituted international jury the Club of Budapest also selects and honours projects of self-help development that embody planetary consciousness. [1] These projects serve as shining examples for practical grass-roots initiatives the world over. The Club does more than just identify and honour such projects; as we now report, it has developed a way for actively supporting their implementation.

The 'Change-the-World' Ethical Investment Fund

Together with the Austrian Partner Bank, an institution that has been designing and marketing ethical financial products for some years, the Club of Budapest has created the 'Change-the-World' Ethical Investment Fund. This basket of shares is limited to enterprises that combine the highest standard of ethics and social and environmental responsibility with dependable financial performance. Investors are assured of the security of their capital whilst being given the opportunity to donate some or all of the interest accruing to them to assist projects awarded the Club of Budapest 'Change the World' Prize.

The Club of Budapest Forum,
The Institute for the Dialogue of Generations and Cultures,
The Mariposa Centre
The Peter Ustinov Centre for the Study of Prejudice

The World Economic Forum in Davos has focused world attention on the economic dimension of globalisation. The Club of Budapest maintains that this emphasis must be balanced by attention to the human dimension of contemporary social and economic activities: values, ethics, social and environmental care and responsibility. Through the above-named forums and centres, the Club of Budapest develops educational and training programmes that help individuals evolve and communicate new ways of thinking and living so that people in all walks of life can be empowered to 'change the world' – to become part of the solution rather than being part of the problem. [2]

NOTES

1. In order to better understand the immense and as yet largely unexploited potential for self-initiated and self-help change toward a humane and sustainable world, we present here the four winners of the 'Change-the-World Award 2002':

The Women's Empowerment Programme in Nepal
The pilot project in Nepal has empowered 130,000 women to found small businesses and

village banks. The result: no less than 75,000 small businesses, 1,000 village banks and 100,000 social projects. Income rose by 800% in 3 years, while the costs per participant has been 25.

The School for Development FUNDAEC in Columbia
At a fraction of the cost of training Western development workers, 50,000 local and highly competent development workers have been successfully trained through this schools' totally new educational system, called by the jury of the world exposition EXPO 2000 "currently the best education project in the world".

The *Trash into Art* Project Reciclar-T3 in Brazil
The Brazilian artist Aguida Zanol trains rubbish collectors to see rubbish as a raw material for furniture and other things useful in daily existence. She also teaches them to use this extaordinary raw material to create works of art that bring a price and increase the quality of their life as well as their self esteem.

New Families for Orphans: The Child Assistance International of Russia and the USA
The mission of the Frank Foundation is to find families in Europe and North America for orphans in Russia, Georgia and the Ukraine. The adopting families are encouraged to forge lasting links with the country of the child's origins, its culture and its language.

2. Further information on the Club of Budapest and its activities is available on the Club's homepage, www.club-of-budapest.org, together with information on participating in its activities and joining its national chapters in Germany, Italy, France, Hungary, the USA, Canada, Mexico, Brazil, India, China, Japan, and Samoa.

A Concise Guide to Further Reading

Compiled by David Woolfson
Programme Director of the Club of Budapest

Background

Dalai Lama, H.H. *Ethics for the New Millennium*. Riverhead Books 2001.

Gorbachev, Mikhail. *On My Country and the World*. Columbia University Press 1999.

Laszlo, Ervin. *Macroshift: Navigating the Transformation to a Sustainable World*. Berret-Koehler 2001.

Muller, Robert and Roche, Douglas. *Safe Passage into the Twenty-First Century*. Continuum Pub Group 1995.

Strong, Maurice. *Where on Earth Are We Going?* Texere 2001.

State of the World

Hertsgaard, Mark. *Earth Odyssey: Around the World in Search of Our Environmental Future*. Broadway Books 1999.

United Nations Environment Program. *Global Environment Outlook:*

United Nations Environment Programme (Global Environment Outlook Series) Earthscan Publications Ltd 2002.

Worldwatch Institute (Editor). *State of the World 2002*. W.W. Norton & Company 2002 .

Worldwatch Institute (Editor). *Vital Signs 2001: The Environmental Trends That Are Shaping Our Future*. W.W. Norton & Company 2001.

Global Futures

Daly, Herman. *For the Common Good: Redirecting the Economy toward Community, the Environment and a Sustainable Future*. Beacon Press 1994.

Hertsgaard, Mark. *Earth Odyssey: Around the World in Search of Our Environmental Future*. Broadway Books 1999.

Homer-Dixon, Thomas. *The Ingenuity Gap*. Alfred A. Knopf 2000.

Laszlo, Ervin. *The Choice: Evolution or Extinction?: A Thinking Person's Guide to Global Issues*. J.P. Tarcher 1994.

Linden, Eugene. *The Future in Plain Sight*. Penguin Putnam Inc 2002.

Mayor, Federico and Bind, Jerome. *The World Ahead: Our Future in the Making*. Zed Books 2001.

Scheer, Hermann. *The Solar Economy*. Earthscan Publications Ltd 2002.

Wilson, Edward O. *The Future of Life*. Alfred A. Knopf 2002.

Ecological Sustainability

Benyus, Janine M. *Biomimicry: Innovation Inspired by Nature*. William Morrow & Co. 1998.

Brown, Lester. *Eco-Economy: Building a New Economy for the Environmental Age.* W. Norton & Company 2001.

Copley, Anthony / Paxton, George. *Gandhi and the Contemporary World.* The Indo-British Historical Society 1997.

Hartmann, Thom. *The Prophet's Way: Touching the Power of Life.* Three Rivers Press 1997.

Hawken, Paul. The Ecology of Commerce. HarperCollins 1994.

Hawken, Paul / Lovins, Amory and Hunter. *Natural Capitalism: Creating the Next Industrial Revolution.* Little Brown & Company 1999.

Henderson, Hazel. *Building a Win-Win World: Life Beyond Global Economic Welfare.* Berrett-Koehler 1996.

Henderson, Hazel. *Beyond Globalisation: Shaping a Sustainable Global Economy.* Kumarian Press 1999.

Nattrass, Brian / Altomare, Mary. *The Natural Step for Business: Wealth, Ecology and the Evolutionary Corporation* (Conscientious Commerce). New Society Publishers 1999.

Peace and Human Security

Dorn, A. Walter (Editor). *World Order for a New Millennium: Political, Cultural and Spiritual Approaches to Building Peace.* Palgrave 1999.

Ferencz, Benjamin. *Planethood: The Key to Your Future.* Love Line Books 1991.

Herzog, Roman. *Preventing the Clash of Civilisations: A Peace Strategy for the Twenty-First Century.* Palgrave 1999.

Lederach, John Paul. *Building Peace: Sustainable Reconciliation in Divided Societies.* United States Institute of Peace 1997.

Rotblat, Joseph / Bruce, Maxwell & Milne, Tom (Editors). *Ending War: The Force of Reason.* Palgrave 1999.

Schell, Jonathan. *The Fate of the Earth: The Abolition.* Stanford University Press 2000.

Thomas, Caroline. *Global Governance, Development and Human Security.* Stylus Publishers Llc. 2001.

Societal Transformation

Berry, Thomas. *The Great Work: Our Way Into the Future.* Harmony Books 2000.

Elgin, Duane. *Promise Ahead: A Vision of Hope and Action for Humanity's Future.* William Morrow & Co. 2000.

Elgin, Duane. *Voluntary Simplicity.* Quill / William Morrow & Co. 1993.

Goodall, Jane. *Reason for Hope: A Spiritual Journey.* Warner Books 2000.

Harman, Willis. *Global Mind Change.* Berrett-Koehler 1998.

Hock, Dee. *Birth of the Chaordic Age.* Berrett-Koehler 1999.

Hubbard, Barbara Marx. *Conscious Evolution: Awakening the Power of our Societal Potential.* New World Library 1997.

Korten, David C. *The Post-Corporate World.* Berrett-Koehler 1999.

Quinn, Daniel. *Beyond Civilisation: Humanity's Next Great Adventure.* Three Rivers Press 2000.

Ray, Paul and Sherry Ruth. *The Cultural Creatives: How 50 Million People Are Changing the World* Harmony Books 2001.

Russell, Peter. *The Global Brain Awakens.* Element 2000.

The Author

Ervin Laszlo

Ervin Laszlo is one of the world's foremost experts on systems theory and general evolution theory. He is Founder and President of The Club of Budapest, Founder and Director of the General Evolution Research Group, Science Director of the International Peace University of Berlin, Administrator of the Interdisciplinary University of Paris, Fellow of the World Academy of Arts and Science, Senator of the International Medici Academy and Editor of *World Futures*.

Professor Laszlo is the author of thirty-four books including *The Consciousness Revolution, Third Millennium, The Whispering Pond, The Systems View of the World, Macroshift and The Connectivity Hypothesis* to be published in 2003. He is co-author of 9 books and editor of 29 others.

Hungarian by birth, Ervin Laszlo was a professional pianist before becoming a scientist. He lives in Italy with his wife, Carita, and travels all over the world lecturing. In 2001 he was awarded the Goi Peace Award of Japan.

The Publishers

Positive News

Positive News is a quarterly International newspaper. It focuses attention on creative solutions and makes visible the many projects and enterprises that are working towards a sustainable future. It acknowledges and supports people who are making innovative and often courageous changes in their lives to create an improved quality of life for themselves and others. Subscribers also receive an education supplement and a full colour magazine, Living Lightly, which explores in greater depth the issues reported in Positive News. Published in the UK. Current circulation between 75,000 and 100,000 worldwide.

Global News Education Trust (Global NET)

Global NET holds the vision that it can contribute to and help create a more balanced and positive media in the future. It encourages young people who hope to work in the media to look at creative solutions and also provides work experience for students and young people in all aspects of publishing. All this is made possible by its association with Positive News. The Trust publishes youth and education pages within the Newspaper and as a supplement.